I0149635

Faye Thom

In His Presence

The Heart of the Father
Revealed through Inspirational Poetry

IN HIS PRESENCE:
The Heart of the Father Revealed through Inspirational Poetry
Copyright © 2025 by Faye Thom

All rights reserved. Neither this publication nor any part of this publication may be reproduced or transmitted in any form or by any means, electronic or mechanical, including photocopying, recording or any information storage and retrieval system, without permission in writing from the author.

ISBN: 978-1-4866-2750-9
eBook ISBN: 978-1-4866-2751-6

Word Alive Press
119 De Baets Street Winnipeg, MB R2J 3R9
www.wordalivepress.ca

WORD ALIVE
—P R E S S—

Cataloguing in Publication information can be obtained from Library and Archives Canada.

Do you enjoy life,
or just go through the motions?
Are your days without purpose: rise, shine,
work to be done,
To bed early, no time to unwind?
Do you need refreshing? Has your light
grown dim, no fullness within?
Many are going through the motions of life,
No fullness within, nothing to draw on, need
new life within.
We all have days with much to be done,
But refreshing is needed.
Dry and thirsty,
we must drink of the life within.
When we are running on fumes, our tank has
run dry, nothing more to give.
Exhausted and tired, teach us to draw from
the well of your life within.
Lord, teach us to live
in your fullness each day.
Take time to draw from the well of life,
A busy world, pressures of life,
We need your fullness to inspire, to fill our
days with joy and abundance.
Thank you, Lord.
Fill our dry vessel with abundant life,
we pray.

Bittersweet

I came to the fountain thirsty;
dry and thirsty was I that day.
When at the fountain I met Jesus,
the master, sitting.
As from the fountain I drew,
I knew he was different.
He said he knew of the days my life passed by,
He knew of the times husbands had I.
He knew I could not deny nor refuse to drink,
thirsty was I.
"If you draw from my well, you shall never thirst; living
waters quench your thirst."
Life-flowing waters of love, then I knew.
I ran to the city.
"Come see," I tell of a man who knows all about me.
My life he knew. I was thirsty.
Said to me a fountain of life that never runs dry;
You'll never be dry thirsty if you draw from me. You'll
never thirst.
Come to the waters; drink of me.
The fountain of life, child, never bitter, sweet.
Never cursing, envy, or jealousy,
Only the sweet water of Jesus's love
flowing through thee.
Out of your belly, waters of life flow,
from the depth of your spirit.
Hear him say, "Come, drink of the water, I pray."
Pure and clean, holy the life of Jesus
flowing through thee.

The life of the master, living sweet waters of Jesus,
never bitter.
Sin may abound, seep through the ground,
tainted water.
Like salt, the water bitter, fountain of cursing,
a fountain of sin.
If you are thirsty and fail to think, *Should I taste of the
water? I need a drink.*
Check the fountain; heed what it says: This water is
bitter and filled with lead.
Now the sweet water of Jesus, drink as you will.
Nothing to hurt you, drink your fill.
Drink till your full.
Give of the water as others come your way.
Say, "Come to this fountain; the water is sweet.
"The Lord is the fountain; come to this fountain, from
the other stay away."
While in desert thirsty, which fountain
will you drink from:
Bitter fountain of sin, death drink in, or the water of life
from the fountain of life?
There are two fountains; you must decide.
People line up thirsty and dry.
Some push and shove as they wait in line,
not knowing the water or the kind.
Water of life, sweet, coming from Jesus,
flowing through thee.
Drink of his water if thirsty, sweet waters of life
flowing through thee.
Do not drink of that fountain bitter. Get out of that line;
don't drink this time.
Cup of sin don't drink in.
Don't drink of that water filled with sin.

Do not take; your cup you best break.
Do not drink.
Stop, child, stop and think: Is the water pure and
clean? Is the water what it would seem?
Does it come from a good stream? Drink of the water
that comes from the rock.
Drink of the water, never stop.
When you are thirsty, when you are dry, come drink of
the fountain that never runs dry.
A fountain of life that flows out water
to nourish and sustain.
Drink of the water that comes from the rock. Drink
from the fountain that never stops.
Drink of the sweet water,
filled and replenished, child.
Come to the river of life; may it flow and fill thee sweet
and pure.
Fill your cup, child. Drink up—
do not go away dry, I pray.
Do not go away thirsty this day;
drink of the water of life each day.
Draw from its well every day, well of life in your soul,
filled with his life as rivers flow.

Scripture reference: John 7:37–39; James 3:8–17

The day before us, what will it bring?
We have an agenda,
but what says the King?
King Jesus perhaps has a plan: things you need to be
aware of, give attention to,
think about.
Schedule in a time to inquire
of the Lord's agenda.
Jobs, chores, responsibilities, children—many things
on our agenda
What says the Lord? Does he have a battle plan for the
day?
Should we take time to inquire
about his plan?
Love will lead through each day,
its challenges.
Help us to respond by spending our awaking hour in
his presence to prepare
for the day ahead.

Awake with Jesus

Rise in the morning, let the sun kiss
your cheeks.
Rise in the morning, hear the Lord speak.
Today is a new day.
You are found in my love, blessed with the spirit life
from above.
In the morning, seek Jesus the Master;
he'll lighten the load, carry thee.
Today is a new day—rise.
He'll carry your burden, child, set you free.
The dawn of a new day, his life seek.
Rise in the morning! Jesus calls:
"Come to my presence.
Take time to worship; dwell with me.
Rise in the morning, spend time with me.
The day before you, what will it bring?
Joy or sorrow, what sort of things?"
Angels minister to your every need;
they are waiting the word to heed.
Faith in his love, faith in the Word,
faith in Jesus. Angels hear—they move that mountain,
battle, bring deliverance.
As the Word flows,
they make war on your enemy.
They heed the word of the Master,
engage in the conflict, battle. Angels fight, devils flee.
Sound the trumpet. Blow the horn.
Prepare for battle. Enter the fight.
Stand on the Word; dwell in the light.

Move in the Spirit; move with the Lord.

He is your captain. Draw the sword.

He goes with you. Stand on the Word.

Jesus the victor draws the sword.

The Lord does battle; we stand on the Word.

Angels hearken to the voice of the Word. Battle, see

the power of Jesus, his army.

Open the floodgates of heaven;

look to the Master.

Engage in the battle, follow.

Angels minister and devils flee.

You are in a conflict. No victory see, only the mountain

in front, only the

mountain standing.

Command that mountain! Cast it

into the sea!

Go forth in Jesus, go forth.

Move in the Spirit; command devils to flee.

You have been purchased; his blood flowed,

victory gained when he hung on the tree.

Devils and demons defeated.

There in the heart of the earth the keys were taken.

Deliverance, the keys of the kingdom,

life bought for thee.

I'll wake in the morning, Jesus seek.

I'll wait on the Master as he talks with me.

I'll dwell in his presence, dwell close,

hear the voice of the Master. Enter the battle; his voice

speaks.

"Child, do battle, command demons to flee.

I am your captain; I'll lead.

Fight like a soldier in my army.

Deliverance was purchased.

Come, do battle; command devils to flee."
Rise in the morning, talk with thee.
He will lead and guide.
The day before you, what will it bring?
Joy or mourning, what awaits?
Enter the battle; give no place for the enemy to attack.
Strong you must be. Watch, be ready;
come, pray.
In me is your strength, your liberty.
Come, do battle, prepare.
Rise in the morning. Rise, be ready
for battle,
prepared, ready to fight the enemy.
His plan of attack you cannot see,
so dwell with the Master and
deliverance see.
Rise in the morning, dwell with thee.
He will guide. Prepared a soldier in
battle guided.
Rise, deliverance was purchased.
Rise in the morning, do battle.
He bought deliverance.
Rise, see the deliverance of your Lord,
his salvation.

Scripture references: Mark 11:23; John 15:5; 2 Corinthians
10:3–5; Ephesians 6:10–20; James 4:7, Psalm 103:20–21, 107:6.

Are you prepared for a power outage, no lights,
the city dark?
Do you fumble to find a candle, a flashlight, stumble?
Have you walked down a dark road, no light to guide?
How difficult, scary, the night can be—not knowing
what lies ahead.
We are the lights in a dark world and must shine bright,
bring others light.
Does your light shine, does love flow?
Is love the goal?
Lord, help us to be the light in the midst of darkness.

Children of Light

Do not put in a drawer nor hide your light; there is a time of darkness in the land. I need you to give of the light I have given, set on a hilltop that others may see the mercy of Jesus, the kindness of the Master. A light set on a hill, light in the night, a glowing ember one can see. Hide not your light, my children, under a bushel, hidden, no light others see. You spoke of your love—move in love, move in me. Dwell in my presence, a light be. Hide not your light, let others see. You spoke of your love, then hide not the light I have given.

Lord, help me hide behind the cross of Calvary, walking with Jesus hidden, set back, humble as Jesus, his life in me. No glory, no crown I seek—only to listen as I sit at your feet, my life a light until dawn breaks. The return of the Master shall come, his glory revealed. What a day that shall be! Angels of heaven riding with thee. The return of Jesus—what a day that will be. Come, saints; come, children, let's dwell in the light. There is gross darkness; we are the light. A light on a hilltop, a city of lights, we'll shine for the Master, we'll dance in the night. We light up the darkness as he lives in us—power of Jesus, power of love.

The lights of the city shall shine, glow in the darkness, bright, full of the Son, full of his light. An ember for Jesus he is our light. Empowered with his love, we'll shine in the night. We his children we are the lights. Set on a hilltop, we shine, break through the darkness, dispel the night. Counselled, filled with his life, each day full of the Word and the Spirit we pray. Full of Jesus, his light. Shine bright, glow in the darkness, dispel the night. Glow with his love; be a light for the Master as he lives. Shine bright; dispel the night. The light of Jesus, his light living in thee; the life of Jesus, your choice to be. A light for Jesus, bright his life, his love flowing through. Jesus, the light of life.

Embers, Jesus breathes, ignites a flame, a burning light you shall be as the breath of the Master he breathes on thee. Ignite a flame; burn in me. Jesus, Redeemer, help me be a flame for Jesus to light the darkness—shine. Bright light, Jesus in me. The light of my life: Jesus, redeemer, friend, master, Lord, I pray he be.

Master of life calling, times of darkness Jesus speaks. When looking for answers, his face seek; meek and lowly, come sit at his feet. He is waiting to comfort you, a friend waiting, calling, reaching. Do not hardened your hearts, mock love; Jesus is beckoning. Many will mock, laugh, scorn, hearts hardened, hearts torn. Walls of hate and fear need the love of the Master to heal. I know you have been hurt. I know you have cried; I have seen your hurt tears you hide. Children, set aside your pride. Bow in my presence; I'll be at your side. I'll carry your burden, heal all the scars. Like a child at play with a handful of cars, you wander in darkness, hearts full of scars. I am asking you, child, for all of your cars; empty-handed, listen as I speak. Take time to listen, your attention I'll keep. Now listen, children, I heal all the scars; after that, children, I give you new cars. Cars are symbols of a child at play. Enter into the game, I say.

I am the Master. I set the play; the rules are laid down in the game. Listen closely, take time to pray. The course is for heaven, Jesus the way. The price of entrance, come sit on his lap. Jesus the King, he drew the map. The first turn you come to is salvation. Enter through Jesus; he is the key. Mercy and love travel the road. Friends, neighbours, passengers on course for heaven: watch the road—rocky, rough may be. Jesus travels with you, moving in love; the way is he. Our map to heaven, the Word, set on a course of love. The fuel of the Spirit will propel, fueled by his love, Jesus. Watch, be ready, rough road, watch for pitfalls, guided by love, smooth roads— the road to heaven begins with thee. You have a choice to hear his voice. Enter the race, or give place? Enter the race or give place. Lay down your toys; your attention, give. A life with the Master your chance to live.

Scripture references: Matthew 5:14–16, 7:13–14, 16:27, 24:30

Do we make wise choices with our day?
Time passes, we cannot recoup, relive, time precious.
The day gone. Did we make the most of the day? Did
we stop to pray for others?
Who knows how the day will end,
Or when we will have another chance to make
a difference.
Did we seek the Lord, his counsel for the day?
Lord, give us your wisdom, guidance.
You know what each day holds; help us to be wise and
value our time.
Time is precious. Let's not squander it away.

Eternity Awaits

Lord, I wait for your wisdom to fill me,
understanding, mercy must flow through,
washed and cleansed, from sin set free.
Endued with power, my life;
hid mercy and truth flow forth—
understanding and wisdom, Lord, I need.
You see the portrait; I see the cloth.
You see the beauty my eyes cannot behold. Lord, help
me be submissive, colour me bold.
Bold is the colour on the canvas you spread,
vibrant with beauty, colour it red.
I'll wave the canvas so all can see;
I'll fly the flag, help others to see
as the flag is raised for thee.
The coloured canvas, red it might be.
Bold is the colour you choose for me.
Boldness comes from the Spirit—bold, not ashamed,
Lord, help me to be.
I'll speak the truth as you lead;
bold like Peter, Lord, may I be.
Spirit of God flow through me—a witness bold.
Help me, Lord, not to be ashamed or afraid to let
others see;
ashamed for what I could not see, afraid of man that
person I be.
Afraid of the ridicule, Lord, afraid to acknowledge the
Lord in me.
I give you my will—help me.
I choose life; I choose thee.

I stumble and fall, scrape my knees;
Lord, you bent down; your love bandaged me.
You pull me up; I sit on your knee—no longer afraid,
your arms around me. You ease the hurting now, I see;
love lifts me up and love carries me.
Why should I fear what men might say?
Why should I tremble? Help me, I pray,
to fear not men.
Do you approve of my way? Did I acknowledge you,
Lord, today?
Did I boldly speak? Was I willing to walk your way?
Someone is hurting; life has been lost.
Someone is crying—they have lost a loved one so
precious; consider the cost.
Torn are their hearts—who can mend?
Taken from them, life did end.
Their child gone into eternity; loved ones left—Lord,
help them.
They need your help; they need thee.
Loved ones torn, broken. Hearts hurting—cause them
to see.
Children, gifts I give to thee.
Jesus the Word was given; he paid the price
for eternity.
He paid for your fare; came, healed, delivered—from
sin set free.
Jesus, the child given for thee.
Heart of the Father, torn, gave his Aon to hang
on the tree.
Gave a child, his gift; gave a loved one—wanted thee,
gave his Son.
Now the time has come: your loved one gone
into eternity.

IN HIS PRESENCE

Your loved one taken, no longer with thee.
Heart of the Father reaches; he understands all.
Your gift so precious—gone, hurting and lonely child;
Jesus of Nazareth reaches, his love extended
—he sustains.
Mercy, Jesus calls, come and behold all he can be.
Come, take hold—he reaches,
carries your burdens, helps.
Lord God Almighty truly loves thee.
Lord, I hear you calling out my name.
Lord, will I ever be the same?
Someone taken—my heart in pain, hurting and crying
as I call on your name.
My heart torn; my life has changed. I see the eternal
through the pain.
My hope and vision, to see them again.
I see my children as I look through the pain.
Is there rejoicing around your throne? Is there joy as a
child comes home?
Help me, Lord; I feel so alone.
Alone and helpless, I am only a man. I need your
strength; give me your hand.
Alone and helpless, I am only a man.
I hear your voice as I look through the pain:
tears and heartache—so much pain; help me, Lord,
understanding gain.
Cause me, Lord, to see through the pain; dry my
tears—I am a child in pain.
Your hand in mine, you take the reins. Lead me and
guide me out of this pain.
Rain and showers come to me; I need your love
—hurt I be.

I need the warmth of your love to bring healing
draw me.
Around your throne in eternity is there my loved one
sitting with you,
your arms around him I am asking you? My heart is
torn is he with you?
Can I be sure your love saw him through?
Did I mention his name in prayer? Did I call when no
one seemed to care?
Did I ask you to bear? Did I carry my loved one to you
in prayer?
My heart was full of cares—did I remember my loved
ones in prayer?
Did I take the time to mention your name? Did I speak
of Jesus, as a babe you came?
Did I take the time to ease their pain?
Lord, my life will never be the same.
Did I come to your throne, bow my knee? Did I men-
tion his name when I came to thee?
Did I look in each direction and say, "That's not for me
nor for my loved ones, Lord, turn
me about"?
Submissive and bold that others may see,
colour the cloth, the canvas for me.
Paint in boldness that others may see
Jesus the Lord living in me.

Scripture references: Psalm 147:1–13; Mark 8:34–38; Luke
9:23–27; John 11:25–26; Galatians 6:1–10; 1 Timothy 2:1–8;
Revelation 21:1–7

Do you see beauty in a flower garden? Notice how different, unique, and beautiful each flower is? People are much like flowers: unique, beautiful, each bringing a different expression to life. When in doubt of the Lord and his love and care, look to the gardener who tends, waters, and feeds the flowers. We are God's precious creations. Would not the Lord attend to his garden? Doubt his love and care? Draw close; be refreshed. Lord, we thank you for your loving care. Help us to take notes from the gardener who tends to the flowers.

Dusty Roses

Rose garden, fragrance of flowers,
dark colours, petals soft,
poppies, silver threads,
sprays, bouquets, flower beds.
A mound, a mountain covered in colour,
deep purple, rich reds—
the beauty of flower beds.
Roses blooming, sun and rain
fresh anointing, nourished again.
Would I not nourish the grass of the field?
Would I not nourish you as you yield?
Tears, sorrow, sad faces—
the limp, the lame run races.
Torn jackets, torn blue jeans,
dusty, dirty—needs to be clean.
Washed in the fountain, a fresh cool spray,
cleansed, anointed day by day.
Flowing waters wash away
the dirty traveller, refreshed each day.
Dusty rose petals fall;
the spray evil, touched by sin,
bend in the wind.
Touched by life, brightens the day,
Nourished, fed on your way.
Choose Jesus—a better way.
Flowers bloom, roses grow,
warmed by the sun.
People need Jesus—he loves each one.
Be a blessing, yield to God's Son.

IN HIS PRESENCE

People, roses, flowers, bouquets,
Beauty, beautiful spray
Nourished, fed by the Master.
Why worry? Yield, pray.
Dusty traveller, stop at the inn,
be refreshed with life again.
Drink at the tavern the water of life;
the well of salvation—draw life.
Dusty roses need rain;
fresh dew revives them again.
Call on Jesus, call on his name.
Come, be refreshed, anointed, blest—
blest each day yield your way.
Stop, pray, seek the Lord his way.
Stop, pray.
Stop, pray.

Scripture references: Psalm 23:1–3;
Isaiah 40:30—31, 58:11; John 6:35

Have you heard the expression, "Such a colourful character" to describes a joyful, lively person full of personality? Light and hearty, or cool and reserved, many different characters we see. Have you ever people-watched to see how different characters catch your eye? Do you marvel, wonder how different, unique, gifted is each man. Thank you, Lord. Paint me the colours of the character that glorifies thee, I pray.

Colour of Love

Lord, go before me, open doors,
give direction, guide—your life in me,
the vision may I see.
Only a glimpse of the picture—you are the painter.
You brush me filled with colour—paint a
beautiful canvas.
You are the artist, a brush covered in love,
mercy-filled.
Hairs on the canvas left by the brush; tares in the
canvas ripped.
You chose the canvas; you chose me,
stretched and straightened on the easel, paint the
picture, beauty.
I wait for the stroke of the brush; work into the canvas
the colour,
paint the canvas, give a coat—covered in love
in every stroke.
Brushed, stroked by the painter's hand,
colours of beauty brushed in your plan.
No life, no colour—just plain,
washed and tattered, rough,
but I am the canvas you chose, tattered and torn,
a rough piece of cloth,
coloured with the brush, tender and soft.
Soft are the bristles that paint me; they brush and they
stroke life into me.
Love is the colour chosen. Love is the paint brushed
into me—
a canvas of beauty as you brush the colour
of love in me.

Blue, the colour bright or faded—Master,
colour the canvas,
colour life into me; blend in the background—can you
see the Master revealed?
Look with your heart; your eye cannot see
nor mind understand.
Jesus the Master revealed—the reflection of Jesus
embossed in the picture, not hidden away;
the reflection of Jesus brushed in.
Washed are the fibres with your blood,
fabric coloured red.
You are the painter—paint, I pray;
paint your colours into the canvas—love, paint.

Scripture references: Psalm 119:73; 139:13–18

A day with no challenges, worries, or stress in life seems impossible. Each day has its own challenges. How we choose to deal with them is up to us. We can choose to pray, trust, believe. Love cares for us, if only we could learn to be like children again—let go of the worries and return to the most precious time of life childhood. Such a wonderful, carefree time. May the Lord reawaken the child in you. Have you forgotten the wonder of childhood, free of doubt and the complexities of life? May simple trust and faith guide your day. Lord, help us become like little children again. Let go of our worries; let go, just simply trust and believe. Thank you, Lord, for your love and care. Help us to trust the wisdom of our creator.

Bubbles and Bubblegum

The funny side of life—simple things
and events of the day
can be used to bring great revelation
and understanding to one's self.
True wisdom and insight
is not always found in great novels,
under great teachers,
or in lectures that have taken
great amounts of study and preparation.
The simple things of life
can be used to open great revelations to man.
For even a fool can find wisdom
if perchance he would listen and learn.
The sun rises the sun sets—simple.
The dawn breaks, the night awaits:
new day, new revelation, new understanding.
How very simple—not complex.
If you are looking for understanding and wisdom,
look to the Lord who created all,
understands all, comforts all.
The need to search is no farther
than a thought away, a call in prayer,
a moment to listen.
Children, bubblegum bubbles,
no thought for tomorrow,
no concern for the day.
The cares of life so far away,
so unaware of the world out there—
so full of life, no envy, no strife.

IN HIS PRESENCE

Blowing bubbles, careless,
no worries to dampen the day.
No worries, no cares,
unaware of life's trouble—
light in heart, happy.
Why do we worry and fret,
struggle to believe
that love cares for you?
No food for tomorrow, bills to pay,
the cares of the world, the stubble, the hay.
Daybreak—the storm recedes.
The work not finished, more storms will come.
But trust like children;
have some fun.
Blowing bubbles like dreaming dreams—
some burst, the truth seen.
Children laugh and try again:
another bubble, bigger perhaps then the first.
Try again when bubbles burst;
come to the Lord, let him quench your thirst.
Drink again from the river of life;
be filled, overcome in life.
When dreams die and bubbles burst,
return to the Lord—let him quench your thirst.
Have you taken time to rest,
Rejoice, and know you will be blest?
For dreams die, people cry—
be like children, cease not to try.
For tomorrow the sun shall rise,
a fresh new start—open your eyes.
A better plan for the whole man.
Why worry, fret, as you do?
Trust the Lord who cares for you.

Be like children: trust, turn, yield your way.
Know that love watches over you.
Trust the Lord in all you do;
let joy unspeakable fill you.
Trust the Lord in all you do;
let joy unspeakable fill you.
Bubbles, bubblegum—
the child in you.

Scripture references: Matthew: 6:25–34; Luke 12:22–31; Philippi-
ans: 4:6–7

IN HIS PRESENCE

Do we realize how important time in prayer is? Wisdom comes from the Lord. He knows the hearts of men. We may miss many opportunities to bless another through word or deed if we don't take time to pray. Each day has its pitfalls and struggles; depend on the wisdom of the Lord to bless a word in season for the hurting. Take time out to pray.

Is prayer of great importance or value? Do we understand the difference prayer can make? We are blessed when we take time out to pray. Hear what the Spirit would say; receive his counsel. Lord, help us submit, yield our will each day. We are blessed to be a blessing.

Direct My Way

Your day gone by— did you stop to pray?
Rise, wait, hear me say?
Were you busy, child? Child, take time to pray.
I desire you to come, sit awhile; climb upon my knee.
I desire to dwell in thee. Come, child, sit, talk.
Rise, start your day; humble yourself and pray.
The day goes by—no longer any time to pray,
no longer any time; the hours have passed away.
Were you near? Did you see the need?
Were your ears open? My voice did you heed?
I have a plan; come follow, dwell in me—I will speak.
I sent one to meet with you,
but you did not hear me, child.
I saw the need; I knew the heart.
I sent that one to you this day. Dwell, child, in me;
pray, heed my voice, my Spirit.
I sent someone your way.
No time to listen, no time to pray—child,
I sent someone your way.
I hear the cry of the heart. Time in prayer, child: spend
time with me; dwell—I will speak.
I will send the lonely, the lost and discouraged,
no word of life, the forgotten bound in strife,
the needy child.
Can I send someone to thee? Can I send a friend,
your hand lend?
Can I send someone to you? Child, can they come
your way?

Will you take the time to pray? Can I count on you to
speak, to lend your ear and lean on me?
Move, child, closer—life passes;
move closer each day.
Move in me—I'll show you the way.
I'll send someone your way,
a word to speak, a need to meet. Can I send someone
your way? Will you take time to pray?
I encourage you: give today of the life in you—
give away.
A word, a prayer, life—give away.
Forgive me, Lord—I did not pray. I did not submit my
will today,
nor did I yield to your way. I was busy and
did not pray.
Pray without ceasing; pray every day.
No time to get quiet—no time; I was busy,
no time to yield.
I did not submit my will nor take time to pray,
nor did I wait to hear.
I did not listen; went my own way, filled with the cares
of life, too busy to pray.
Bought, purchased with your blood—child of light,
child of love,
child unwilling to yield this day.
Submit unto me—I am he. Submit in love;
bow your knee.
You can do nothing apart from me. I am the vine—
abide in me.
Supplied by the roots, nourished and fed,
child filled from toe to head.
Full of light, my love shed. Yielded and filled,
let your life be.

I ask you to choose and bow your knee, a life of sub-
mission to your God Almighty.
Lord, I saw a loved one today; remembered the words.
I can still hear her: words to direct my way, words of
direction for me that day, words of wisdom
came my way.
When I was young, she would say, "Child, you should
go to Sunday school; remember the golden rule."
Words of life to direct my way. Though I was young,
I still hear them.
Did you stop and listen today? Did you take time out
to pray?
A word of life—did I give today, or did I go about
my own way?
Discouraged, disheartened souls far from Jesus, gone
astray—take time out to direct their way.
Take time out to stop and pray. The course of life you
can change—direction given, light.
Direction spoken, a hand given—love will alter the day,
heal the hurts, wipe tears away.
Child, give of your life each day. Take time out—
go pray.
Living yielded, life pouring through—giving to others.
Filled and flowing, giving to others, the needy. Praise
the Lord, the battle's won.
God eternal gave his son. Jesus came—no one to
blame.
The choice is yours; call on his name.
Life direction, love poured out, flowing through—child,
the life of the believer submitted each day. Come,
bow, pray; your will yield. Come, bow, pray—Jesus
the Master; hear him: he knows you are busy.
Someone needs help through this day—guidance,

direction, a smile. Can I send this one your way? Did
you listen, take time to pray? Can I send the lonely, the
needy your way? Will you take time to pray?
Will you dwell in my presence, spend time each day?
Will you give to the needy I send your way—a word, a
song to help along, lift up the downcast, the outcast?

Direct him to Jesus; love him, I pray. Needy and
helpless, many bound in sin, no chance to win. Lend a
hand—make a friend by your love; draw them in, hold
on to the needy; give life pouring from you each day.

Give to the needy as they pass your way: a hand, a
smile, words of life—no anger, hate, bitterness, strife.
A brother, a sister on the road of life—lend your hand,
end the strife. Help someone on the road of life.
Lend a hand, give today; give to the one I send your
way. Child, listen—come, pray.
Give of the life to someone each day. On the road of
life help the needy, downcast—lend a hand,
be a friend.
Draw that brother, sister into the fold safe. Lend a
hand, give a smile, walk a mile—kindness and love
cover them.
Ask for forgiveness for their sins; mercy and love cov-
er. I will draw them unto me. Do for them; a friend be.
A friend closer than a brother—Jesus is he; there
through adversity, laid down his life.
Jesus, your friend he will be.
Someone falling, hurt—they have stumbled; they need
a friend to help; they need Jesus—he is the way.
Can I send them your way? Will you help? Will you
pray? Can my life flow through you?
Can it reach out from you?

Are you willing to lay aside, yielded still in me—your
will hid? Yielded still you must be.
You must yield your will.
Someone hurts—can I send them your way? Will you
encourage, take time to pray?
Yield your will to me this day? A word, a voice for me
each day, flowing through the pot of clay. Yielded on
the wheel—lay, let me mold the pot of clay; formed
and molded every day.
Yielded on the wheel, let me form the clay. Can I send
a child your way? One is lost, hurt—can I count on you
to yield as I mold the clay?
Yielded child, let me mold the clay. Let me help you to
pray, teach you from the Word each day.
I know how, what to pray. Yield your will to me; pray in
the Spirit, pray without ceasing—call,
speak with me, child.
Let me live in you—yielded a vessel of clay, formed by
the Master's hand. Pot of clay, form this day; yielded
on the wheel I lay.
Formed by the Master, his love displayed. Formed in
beauty as you lay—I form the vessel, mold the clay.
Yield your life—yield, pray. Submit your will each day.
Life goes on; no time to recover the broken clay.
Listen, child, yield your life each day. Still on the wheel
lay; the potter forms the clay.
Can I send someone your way? Did you listen? Did
you pray? Are you yielded? Give of the life— Jesus the
way—direct to the Potter who forms the clay.
Let the love of Jesus shine through—yielded is the
clay. Life of Jesus fills each day, flowing through
the child at bay,
flowing through yielded, touching someone.

Love of Jesus flowing through the pot of clay.
Yielded on the wheel, life, love fill your day. Child, all
on the alter lay.

Scripture reference: Isaiah 64:8; John 15

We are by nature drawn to many things and repulsed or put off by other things—like insects are drawn to the light, flies to honey, bees to sweet scents. Many others things in nature draw or repel. Do you find yourself drawn to beautiful gardens—the fragrance, the colours, the beauty? Or drawn to kind and joyful people? Kindness draws, while mean, cantankerous people we chose to avoid. Words can open our hearts, let down our guard. A kind word is truly a drawing card; harsh words and judgements cause one to draw back amd avoid those people and situations. Should we be so fortunate to learn to love, be kind. Be like Jesus—loving, giving, and sharing the beauty of his life. Full of joy, generosity, and kindness—walking in his wisdom. What a blessing that would be! Many need the sweet fragrance of love that lives in us.

Fragrance of Heaven

Life is like the flower
that blooms in the spring,
with the fragrance of heaven as he breathes,
the beauty of Jesus as he lives,
the love of the Master as he flows.
Through the beauty of Jesus,
may he bloom in me.
Like the beauty of roses,
the Lord is the sweet rose of Sharon—
Jesus is he.
The fragrance of love draws.
When you look on the flower, its beauty, joy—
beauty he brings.
Rose of Sharon, beauty;
Lily of the Valley, Jesus is he.
Fragrance of heaven flowing—
Jesus, Saviour, precious is he.
Rose of Sharon, love calls.
Lily of the Valley, holy is he.
Fragrance of heaven drawing.
Crimson roses—his blood flowed for thee.
Lily of the Valley, washed, cleansed.
Fragrance of heaven drawing,
gentle breath of Jesus as he breathes.
Master, Redeemer, Friend calling from heaven:
"I will nourish thee."
Beauty of lilies white,
beauty of roses crimson.
Savior, Redeemer—Jesus is he.

Holy God of heaven, may he breathe on thee.
Fragrance of Jesus, his love fills thee.
Holy God of heaven, a rose is he;
Rose of Sharon, his beauty we see.
Lily of the Valley, the cross purchased thee.
Tears and sorrow, he paid for thee,
purchased your redemption; precious you be.
Like the flower on the hillside, his beauty we see;
like the rose of Sharon in the garden is he.
Lily of the Valley—a tender plant was he.
Nourished and fed by the Master are we.
Like the dawn of a new day, Jesus calls.
Rise in the morning, his beauty see,
in the ray of sunshine as the dawn breaks,
in the warmth of his love, in the fresh morning dew.
Awake with Jesus—his life in you.
Awake with the Master and the morning dew,
fresh breath of heaven to nourish, feed, to live in you.
The dawn of a new day, Jesus wakes with you.
Like the dew on the roses, he washes you.
With the dawning of daybreak, the Lord beckons.
Lily of the Valley, beauty—the gentle kiss of heaven is
the dew;
the fragrance of Jesus is drawing you.
Beauty of Jesus, beauty anew.
Fragrance of heaven drawing you.
Dew on the roses, love kisses you.
Wind in the valley breathes on you.
Breath of Jesus dries the dew;
cleansed and washed, love calls you.
Like the Rose of Sharon or the Lily,
the love of Jesus beckons.

IN HIS PRESENCE

Call of heaven—oh, the morning, dew-washed and
cleansed with his life.
Precious is Jesus, his love anew.
Like the Rose of Sharon, love calls,
drawn by beauty, his love.
Kissed by the morning as the day awaits,
the beauty of Jesus calls.
Life is like the flowers reaching to the sun.
Life is like the rosebud, life just begun,
warmed in the sunshine, kissed by morning dew,
beautiful and fragrant, giving to you.
The smell of roses, beauty we see—
none is like Jesus; Rose of Sharon is he,
giving to the needy life, fragrance of heaven calls.
Blossoms and flowers—your choice to be,
full of his beauty and fragrance,
Master of heaven, life, Rose of Sharon beauty.

Scripture references: Song of Songs 2:1; Matthew 6:25–34; 2
Corinthians 14–16; Ephesians 5:2

Do you think of yourself as being like a diamond, beautiful and rare, or just a pebble kicked on the ground? With spit and polish we clean up, rubbed and scrubbed, words we say. Consider yourself a precious stone the Lord polishes and hones. Dear Lord, you are the rock in us. Help us to shine bright—your brilliance we need.

Facets of Wisdom

Facets of wisdom, much like a gem,
beauty of love reflected in men.
The pearl a rare stone, smoothed and polished,
by the oyster honed. Honed jewels, polished
each day;
the crown example is Jesus, the Way.
The prime concern is to yield, learn;
correction do not spurn.
I polish my children, I polish each jewel,
many lessons as I disciple you.
Wisdom must fill you, and wisdom must check you.
Does another stumble because of me?
Say, "Lord then correct me."
Say, "Jesus, create in me the facet of wisdom that
glorifies thee."
Facets, jewels, shine in the sunlight,
sparkle like diamonds.
A glow in a dark place, a candle, a light—
a soft reflection of radiant light.
A burning fire, heat that refines;
a furnace of fire—heart refined.
A facet of Jesus kindled each time,
and embers of self die in time.
Die each day to your way so the crown jewel
may reflect in you
all the wisdom that you need, so to self concede.
Pull back from the pride trap;
in Jesus nothing you lack.

Facets of Jesus, his wisdom in you, will be an
example for others too.
Be an example of a submitted life, and carry your
cross—ease your strife.
Be an example of a committed life and submit to
correction of his holy life.
Follow sound advice. Yield to Jesus
to harvest the fields.

Scripture references: Proverbs 3, 8

Time passes quickly; we are busy work: families, time spent pursuing our particular interest, whether sports, travel, business pursuits, or the many adventures life offers. So much time engaging in worldly events, forming relations, friendships that last for a lifetime. Life passes, and before we know it, old age creeps up on us. My question: Was there time for Jesus, time spent in his presence to become your most precious friend? Did you take time out of your day to pray, talk with the Lord, walk? How can you get to know someone unless time is spent with them? How much time do we set aside to talk, dwell with the creator who gave his life for us? Lord, may we recognize the value of time in your presence—time to learn, listen, be blessed. Thank you for salvation and abundant life—your promise to us, your children.

Friend or Acquaintance?

Come, child—he is calling, reaching; his hand
extended, his love—see.
Mercy and forgiveness are calling. He'll pardon your
sin and set you free.
The cross is the door—Jesus hung there, nailed and
pierced; his blood flowed.
His hand now extended, reaching: "Come, child, I will
set you free."
I know the days set before you; life is precious—
come, dwell.
Many are busy; my light they do not see nor hear my
voice. Child, help them to see.
Jesus is calling; he is reaching out. He is at your side,
though you may not notice.
Unobserved in the background, Jesus is waiting,
reaching arms extended; love is drawing.
The Spirit—gentle, patient—the Master waits.
Busy, so burdened with this life, full of the temporal,
full of our plans.
Busy, yes—busy, no time, no time for his friendship,
no time.
How little we talk, what little we see; how close a
friend can he be.
Friends call each other; they sit, talk, share.
How good a friend is the Master to thee? Laid down
his life for your sin—went to the cross, chose to die.
How good a friend is he? He willed to go so you would
be free. He willed to die on the cross.

How good a friend is Jesus? Did he betray your trust
as you confided in him?
Did he take the time when you came? Did he turn
away when your need he could see?
Child, I ask you—is he a friend? Was he waiting to
help you on the road?
Was Jesus one who would turn from thee? Would he
walk by when your need he could see?
How good a friend is Jesus?
Lord, I am so busy. Lord, can't you see? My life is full
of the temporal; I have plans and desires. Please wait
as I consider—consider whether or not you'll be Lord
of my life or just an acquaintance to me.
A brief hello or friend, a passing fleeting moment in
time or an enduring precious friendship will I have?
Crowded and busy my life—maybe I'll choose to take
time out, choose to sit on your knee.
You knit our hearts together; make a blanket, cover
me—warm and nourish, fill me.
I'll take that blanket, cover the lost, the weary as you
flow out from me.
Fill my cup, my friend; when I am thirsty, you give to
me—fill my cup, then I will be blessed, nourished by
your love. I shall tell others you are the dearest friend.
Friend or acquaintance, what will it be? Knit together
or threadbare?
A tear in the blanket, a hole—child, you will be chilled;
sin will bite, bitten, chilled, sin.
Let me repair and mend. Friend or foe,
what is he to thee?
Embarrassed, ashamed—are you? At the foot of the
table or at the head—where is he?
Did he wash your feet? Was he humble?

Did he offer his cloak? Did he walk a mile with thee?
Did he visit you when you could not see? Did he wait
in the shadows, gently calling?
Did you hear his voice? There in the dark of night was
he? There in the shadow of life waits he.
He looks with mercy, pleading; gentle is Jesus—gentle
is he. Gentle his love and mercy.
He'll wash your feet, pardon; he'll pass by if you
choose not—but with love everlasting he'll wait. Busy,
so busy my life may be. Wait for a moment;
take time to see.
Look in the distance; look close—see the hand of
Jesus reaching out.
There in the shadow of your life is he; there in the
midst of darkness the glimmering of love
his light shall be.
Though a glimmer now, let it radiant be—brilliant, radi-
ant holy; your eyes cannot behold his glory. He is the
King of eternity—brilliant, radiant, the light of God.
The day of judgement will come: rejected or covered
with his love?
Accepted, forgiven, found in thee—or rejected, re-
fused—what will it be?
Friend or foe—who is Jesus to thee? Covered and
forgiven, or rejected?
Blood-washed and cleansed, or sin covering thee?
Forgiven or rejected, friend or foe?
The choice is yours to know a life of fullness or a life of
temporal fullness—what will it be?
Friend or foe, who is Jesus to thee?

Scripture References: John 15:1–15; Proverbs 17:7, 18:24

How magnificent a garden—beautiful, unique each flower, gifted children, creations of love, cared for by the master. Look beyond the natural—see with the eyes of faith the value of each child, the precious soul, the beauty in each creation. Thank you, Lord, for such beautiful souls—creations of love.

Garden Bouquet

Help me to pray, rise early, your face seek.
Gentle and lowly, I sit at your feet.
Gentle the Saviour, kind and meek.
Your mercy covers me; love and forgiveness, the path
sure—he will cleanse, pardon.
Mercy and truth dwell with thee. Move as an army;
speak God's Word in faith.
Nestled in the branches, hid in the tree, close to the
trunk—hid.
Winds may blow; storms may be;
sheltered by the Master's arms around thee.
I awake in the morning; wait to listen for
your voice speak.
I long to hear, draw near, walk through the morning
speaking with thee.
A walk through the garden beauty—each is a flower,
each planted,
positioned by the gardener.
I came to the garden—what would I see?
Flowers vibrant, nourished, beauty, colour all around.
This is a rose, child. Look at the beauty—open petals
warmed by the sun.
Fragrant is the blossom the fragrance draws.
Look—another planting, another bed full
of beauty, different.
Not like the rose but similar; created in love.
Beauty different,
but still drawing life.
Flowers, roses, a garden—colours, shapes different;

IN HIS PRESENCE

some brilliant; others soft.
Some short; others long-stem.
They form a pattern of beauty.
Come, walk through the garden.
One is missing—perhaps two or three—broken and
torn by the wind,
beaten by frost, smitten, beaten down, stripped to the
ground, the beauty wiped away.
Now they need sunshine and water to
nourish the roots.
Cause them to grow again, nourished each day; roots
still intact, growing back their beauty again to display.
A garden: flowers enhance your day, lighten and
brighten, beauty at play.
Dancing in the breezes, kissed by the dew, sheltered—
growing all day through.
Spring and summer beauty, splendour adorned;
the flower, each one in place in the plan—a garden
formed by my hand.
Child-like the garden, each one is placed in the body:
some teachers, ministers, others musicians, called.
Some prophets and apostles; gifts of helps, healings,
miracles of faith found in thee.
Each has a purpose—each different,
but placed by me.
A garden of flowers, a garden much like
the body of believers;
each has purpose and fragrance,
each different beauty.
Clusters of flowers—a bouquet wrapped in love—
nourished.
Drawing from the soil—roots reaching, clinging,
buried in me.

Reaching, spreading out, covered and nourished,
moisture watered by the gardener who cares for thee.
Protected by the rock, sheltered wisdom of the gar-
dener planted thee.
Musicians, minstrels, worshippers, pastors, teachers
prophets, apostles found in me;
Reaching, stretching, growing—warmed by the Son,
arms around thee, fed and nourished the Word.
Covered by the blood; no time to lie down—rise turn
to the Son.
Like the flowers at play, dancing in the breezes as he
blows on your day.
Stretching, growing, moving like the flowers
in the garden;
dancing in the breezes, the sun warms their day.
Stretching and growing, child fed by the Master,
nourished a garden of beauty.
Children at play, dancing in my love—stretching,
growing, not toiling—beauty arrayed.
Solomon in his glory no match, no match for the lily
splendour arrayed.
Beauty—no toiling, no struggling; growing in me much
like the lily, a flower at play.
Come to the garden; see the beauty displayed. Come,
walk every day.
As we walk in the garden, hear me say,
"beauty, splendour all array; children of love, my body,
beauty created, placed.
Come to the garden; I will lead the way, show you the
plan for the day."
Some days there is weeding—the job must be done.
Some need water; others, the sun. Some say they
need more sunshine to warm their day.

Some stand tall, dance in the breeze; others grow low,
cover the ground.
Each draws life. None can say, "No need of the
gardener or his hand."
Short, tall, big, small, vibrant, soft, velvet some—soft
and tender plants.
Strong and hardy, resilient some—what a mixture!
What a bouquet!
Bouquet of beauty, the body growing in love each day.
Growing, not toiling, through the day; garden of
flowers, children at play.

Scripture reference: 1 Corinthians 12:1–31

At times we fail to see the love and kindness of the Lord. We look at the circumstances, clouds, a day without the sunshine. Feelings and emotions flavour the day. We listen to the news—the voices of hate, fear, corruption so prevalent in today's society, drowning out the voice of the Word. In every circumstance and on every occasion, the Word must have first place—our rock in life. Turmoil, fear, tragedy—a world in need of the Word of life to sustain and fill us for each day. None else has the wisdom, power, provision to keep us safe and secure. May we learn to lean rely on Jesus. Help us, Lord, to spend time in your Word and presence.

House on a Rock

I see the riches money can buy; I see the wealth, the
pride of the eye.
Temporal, not eternal—don't trust in them. I'll furnish
you, child, in a world of sin.
I'll give you a cloak to keep you warm, give you shel-
ter, strength in the storm.
I'll furnish you child as you lean on me; together dwell
in unity.
Storm clouds are coming; the days become dark.
Winds and pressures begin to start.
Shaking and moving—will your house stand? is it built
on the rock or on the sand?
The pride of life to many a snare—comforts and
pleasures a world out there.
Many are caught in the turmoil of life, many
heartbroken in strife. Is your foundation based
on the rock?
Is the builder, Jesus, the rock? Is the mortar his
strength, his life?
Storms will blow. Will he see you through? Will he
leave or forsake you?
Will another to you be true? Through the storm, can
he count on you?
Will you acknowledge though you don't see?
Will you give glory your life hid in thee? Will you rely
and depend on him?
The solid rock—Jesus is he. The sands wash away;
the foundation does crack.

Is your life on the right track? Have you built a
foundation secure—built on the rock?
Child, draw near. There are some secrets I would have
you to know.
Someone so special wants you to know
the plan and the purpose he will bestow on the
obedient child.
Obedience brings blessing in your life, ends the
division, heals the strife.
Wait for a moment—partake of life; I have a plan
for your life.
Many are busy, their lives full; many I called to do my
will. Many are chosen; come, be still.
Drink of my Spirit; drink your fill. Draw from the well,
I say to you.
When you are empty, I'll fill you. I call your name,
speak: Come, my child, come be filled.
My Spirit you need; my word you must heed.
You need my blessing; you need me.
Obedience shall bring blessing as you walk with me.
Times of trouble, times of fear—come, child,
come draw near.
I strengthen you; through the valley,
I will walk with you.
Through the valley clouds hide the sun, cover the sky,
no light you see—lean on me.
I part the waters; I am he. I part the cloud, silver the
lining now seen.
Through the valley, walk with me;
through every storm, lean on me.
Though the passage narrow may be, narrow the way
of truth. Narrow the pass—not a highway. Sometimes
it is rough; you must be tough. Tough in my strength.

IN HIS PRESENCE

Expressions only, the humble shall walk with me.
Only the meek, pure shall see the glory of God
as he lives.
Child, I am calling, waiting. I send love to draw thee:
Teachers, pastors, my body teaching and preaching
the Word.
Lay down your plans; come, sit awhile. Come, be
wise—look at the skies.
Come, draw near; I shelter you. I cover my children,
watch over you.
Hide in the shadows of my love. Dwell in my presence,
God of love.
Sheltered and protected from the storm—
in my presence, child, be warmed.
Warmed with my love, touched by my heart. Heart of
the father the Spirit imparts.
Word of God in every part of your life, filling your heart.
Do not stray from my presence, child; come, pray.
Know me—know my way. Know the heart of the father
each day.
Come, child, come.
Love letter written to you this day. Word of God
passes your way.
Acknowledge the truth, the life, the way.
Jesus, life-giver, will deliver from the storm each day.

Scripture references: Psalm 119:10–52; Proverbs 21; Matthew
7:24–29; Luke11:28

The natural, our five senses—what we see hear, smell, taste, and feel—is how we gain our perspective in life. With spiritual eyes, we believe in what we can't see, feel, or touch. Our natural man can't comprehend the things of the spirit. We live out our lives from the natural perspective. May the Lord awaken us to the Spirit life, to live being full of the Spirit. Thank you, Lord. May we be born again of the Spirit and live according to your Spirit, your will, Your word. Thank you for the gift of eternal life.

Life's Card

Marvel not, child of mine, your hand in mine,
marvel not, your life in mine.
Born of the Spirit, life divine,
gift of God, your life in mine.
Born again, free from sin, born this day,
sin washed away.
Into my kingdom come, yield your life to the Son.
Be born again, spirit renew,
born of the life I purchased for you.
Nicodemus did say, "Show me that way.
How can someone again enter the womb?"
Not fleshly birth I speak of,
but birth by the Spirit—the new birth of love.
Marvel not, I will make you my friend.
Marvel not, life will begin, born of my love,
my life in you.
Filled with my life, pardoned.
Come enter in—life everlasting, eternal.
Life, the Holy One has come your way.
Marvel not, come to me.
You will understand as I speak, teach my ways.
I search the heart, take the life you used to live,
replace with my love that others may live.
A new creature, created anew.
The old man has died, reborn by my Spirit,
my life in you—yield, to me be true.
I came for you.
I came to be Lord, God, King, my life in thee.

Nestle in me, surrounded by love,
born of the Spirit, love from above.
No darkness, no vanity, no pride or rebellion
will you see.
Spirit of God—he lives in me, to watch over my life, to
watch over me.
Come to the waters, drink.
Yield your members; come, walk my way.
Nicodemus, he tried, wanted new life,
could not understand, thought like a man.
In the natural, you see the impossibility.
You only see through the glass, darkly.
Natural man will not understand.
The natural life—a life of strife,
not born of my Spirit, no life, only the natural man.
Reborn again by the Spirit, you reign.
Reborn of my love.
You ask, "How can this be?"
For your eyes cannot see, nor mind comprehend the
plan I send.
I have a plan—I came to man, wanted your love,
wanted you.
I desire your friendship; I came to save, created in
love, man of God.
You chose, away from me you did stray.
You live in fear all of your day,
burdened with cares, fear of death.
Blinded by Satan, god of this world,
deceived and bound, sin all around,
under the weight, no chance to escape.
I came for you, my journey through time, the plan
divine to deliver mine,
my creation from the beginning of time.

IN HIS PRESENCE

I created you—choose life eternal.

What have you to lose? Lost and afraid,
the foundation I laid.

The name of Jesus, the price paid, the blood of the
lamb, God's redemption plan.

His purpose, his life, free of strife.

No sin I see, the blood covers; blood of Jesus
paid for thee.

Now come if you will; come, be filled.

Come to me, my life in thee.

Eternal I say, no other way.

The way and the truth, the bread of life, broken, torn.

Many will scorn; many will heed, many forlorn.

Many people, friends, family, refuse my call, refuse me.

They can't understand the redemption plan, nor do
they see the Lord.

He came to purchase life abundant.

Houses and cars, money and fame, pride and rebel-
lion—all part of the game.

The table is set; come draw a card.

Perhaps you are lucky; perhaps you'll be scared.

The game draws to a close—a winner, who knows?

The price was paid as the cards were laid.

You won the game, you receive fame.

You won the jackpot—the money, the cars.

You were lucky, no apparent scars.

But in the game, did you play fair?

Did you cheat and complain? Did hatred reign?

Were you out for yourself? Did your brother fail?

Did you lend him a hand, help him walk tall?

Did you reach out to see the player beside thee?

Did you look in his eyes as he pulled a card?

FAYE THOM

Now the card he pulled from the deck
you can't shuffle,
there would be a scuffle.
His card will scar, his eyes will show,
this card of life he'd rather not know.
Card of disappointment, a card of fear,
a card of defeat, of suffering and pain—emotions are
torn again.
A card of hate, what a fate.
Sin and disease, the card you see.
You were lucky; life was good, happy—until the last
card you drew.
The last card determines your fate; though you were
lucky, reality waits.
You may fold, lay down your cards;
give all to Jesus, the healer of scars.
Give all to Jesus; he will pardon you.
Life of the Master waiting for you.
Hold in your hands, the gamble is yours.
Pick up the deck—oh, what the heck!
Can it be true, will I be lost too?
The gamble is mine; I still have time.
Another round, perhaps one more chance
before eternity.
Do you believe life is in your hands? Given a choice to
enter God's plan.
The fate you choose, the cards in your hands.
Shall you lay down, fold the hand?
Life eternal purchased for thee.
Come now, my children, I truly love you.
Come to me, see—I have one purpose, holy it be.
I am one God—Jesus, Father, Spirit, one in thee.
Come, take my hand; enter my plan.

IN HIS PRESENCE

Victory is yours; come enter the land.
No tears, no sorrow, all scars healed,
filled with my Spirit, to my life yield.
Come draw nigh, I watch over you.
Life eternal comes to you.
There is no sorrow, no pain, no hurt; no disease or
sickness can live with me.
Life of the master comes your way—choose to enter
his plan.
Move from the table, lay down your cards.
Life is hard; you have been dealt a bad card.
I'll draw for you, I see through, I draw from a deck,
a new deck.
A deck of love, life, joy, and contentment found in me.
This is the card I have chosen for thee: peace and joy.
Understanding—this is the second card.
Righteousness, holiness, purity—these three cards
come from me.
Love and mercy—the fourth card, chosen with love
when I hung on the tree.
Now the blood of Calvary is seen in the deck—
red, crimson, it glares at thee.
No other card can pay the price.
Each card you choose shall bless your life.
Cards of victory, cards of life—the deck is shuffled;
I choose the pace.
I choose the card that you need.
I am the one who can see beginning to end as you
yield to me.
Let me shuffle. Holy am I.
Yield to my will; yield—be still.
I'll help you; I'll draw for you.
I know you have faith, but do you have love?

FAYE THOM

I know your talents; I know you.
The cards I choose as you yield to me shall cause life
to be built into thee.
Built up in love, faith, and good works, Word of life,
Spirit in thee.
The foundation—none other can be.
I know the deck, and I draw for thee.
I see your sisters, your family, my love and my mercy
watch over thee.
I see the need; my life they heed.
As I love you, I love them too.
All together, my family, people of God, yield to me.
My plan and purpose you shall see.
People of God, yield to me.
People of God, let me be Lord God Almighty,
God to thee.
Provider and friend, my hand I lend to give you life,
a world without strife.
A world of blessing will come from my hand.
People of God, I'll give you the land.
Land of love, where flowers grow.
Warmed by sun, the flower grows.
Each is a flower, a rose.
Beauty—my eyes go over the land,
the fields filled with beauty, love living in thee.
Colours, shapes, different hues make the landscape.
Your choice to partake, to make a picture, a beautiful
scene over the land.
Love, my plan covers the earth, covers its span.
Cards, flowers, whatever you choose—the card, the
deck, how can you lose?
The choice is yours, what will it be?
The life to come—eternity.

Life goes on, I call upon you to choose.
How can you lose?

Scripture references: John 3:1–31, 10:10; 2 Corinthians 8:9;
Galatians 5:22–23

We are so blessed, our lives full of abundance in all things: health, wealth, relationships, the goodness of the Lord. Gifted and blessed! Perhaps an element of pride rises, forgetting that love is our provider, deliverer in all things. Let us not forget to humble ourselves under his hand, knowing that without him, we are lost and needy. Help us not to forget, Lord, that you are the foundation of our blessed lives.

Necklaces

Are your motives pure, holy, child?
Come to my presence; sit awhile under the light
of my love.
I see each blemish, spot, not love.
Take your blood, Lord; wash me—may my motives be
pure holy; cleanse my sin, Lord;
move through the chambers hidden from view.
Dark the chambers—sin lurking within?
Hidden motives, impure, unkind, not worthy to be a
child of thine.
Evil desires—cleanse me; a branch abiding, from this
seed a strong tree.
Cleanse, Lord, the self in me.
Selfish desires, hidden from view—none can see,
only you.
You look in the heart, see every part; cleanse,
Lord, the sin from my heart.
Your motives pure, holy in me. I will make you
a strong tree.
Shade for the needy as I dwell in thee, flowing
in love purity.
Necklace of pride take from me.
You give me gifts more precious. Your hand in mine,
your life in mine;
all that I am is thine.
I wore the necklace of pride. I strutted around
for all to see.
Gifts so temporal came to me; then Jesus the Lord
caused me to see.

The band of the necklace from me did fall—broken;
the beauty I recall, broken in pieces taken away. Then
I looked—saw Jesus the Lord looking at me, his hand
extended, reaching in love;
said, "I gather all the broken pieces.
I give life, much more than bread—living bread.
Gifts of life come—some temporal, others eternal.
I am Jehovah—I provide.
Arrayed like a lily—beauty in you, fed like the grass by
the morning dew.
I rain my love down on you. The necklace you wear—
none can compare,
none so beautiful, given beauty in each glance.
A necklace of love, humility. Put on your jewels;
wear a crown.
Come to the garden; walk around.
See all the beauty in the flower that grows—none can
compare to a child with love flowing through, giving
love all day through, giving moisture like the dew.
Give to others what I give to you. Love—a necklace
placed on you. Love—a mantle covers you.
Love—a gift given; Jesus, Lord, living in you.
Necklace of pride hurts your eyes. Bold and daring,
the necklace glaring,
repels the person who comes to you by your own
hand, taken from you.
Did you acknowledge what I give you? Was it your
own hand that blessed you?
Necklace of pride must fall. Did you acquire by your
own hand, or was it the Lord lending a hand?
Will you acknowledge the one you don't see, giving
and helping, hidden to thee?
When in trouble, did he reach to you?

IN HIS PRESENCE

When overcome, did he call to thee?
When downhearted, filled with grief, was the Master
the one to bring relief?
Did someone pray, bring your name to his throne?
Did you feel all alone?
Was your name mentioned in prayer?
Given to Jesus, the Master does care; you never know
who knelt in prayer.
Compassion was felt; someone did care.
Your name was brought to the throne in prayer; some-
one somewhere did really care.
Now, you might acknowledge this could be true, but
will you let him live in you?
Will you unclasp, let go of your grasp?
The necklace of pride must fall at your side.
Let go of the necklace; let it go.
Jesus, Saviour come—grow in me every day in your
special way;
grow like the flower in beauty arrayed.
Clothed by the Spirit in garments of love, fit for the
Master to dwell, power of love his life in you.
Jesus lives; Jesus gives to equip you.
Love lives in you, love flows through, reaching and
touching your life through.

Scripture references: Psalm 51:1-13; Psalm 73; John 15:1-17;
James 3:13-18; 4:1-10

Iced tea, fresh lemonade,
quenching the thirst on a hot day;
shade tree, a large comfy chair, time to sit, recoup,
relax, lay back.
The heat of summer, the warm air pleasant,
so surrender to the chair.
Refreshed, revived we come alive.
Jesus refreshes our lives.
Remember to come to him each day and receive re-
freshing from the well of life within, the living water.
Sit with Jesus, abide in him, be refreshed each day.
Thank you, Lord, for the pure, sweet waters of life.

Pools in the Desert

Come to the water; come, child, drink.
Come if you are thirsty, draw from me;
I quench the thirsty.
Rivers of living water flow from your being as you
draw from me.
Come, call on me. I water the thirsty; I'll fill thee.
Springs in the desert flowing, times of refreshing,
times of cleansing—the blood flowed for thee. Springs
in the desert, a dry land, wells of refreshing as you
dwell in me.
Pools of washing, cleansed. Come to the water;
I'll fill thee.
A dry land parched—cracks and crevices, holes, hurts
and disappointments, failures.
Come, let me fill you; dry don't be. Pools in the
desert—come, see.
Times of refreshing as you dwell in me;
take your portion, take of the waters if thirsty.
Take of the cleansing in the pool; come to the water,
and I will fill thee.
Twilight in the desert beauty, blossoms on the cactus,
flowers drawing of the moisture.
Precious dew of the evening moisture
in the desert, needy.
Child, you're like the cactus, growing tall and strong,
drawing of the moisture—precious life each day.
Drawing of the moisture that comes your way.
Blossoms in a dry land, pools, times of refreshing as
you dwell in me.

Beauty in a dry land, beauty, drawing from the waters
blessed by me.
Drawing of the water, Jesus is he. Filled with the Spirit,
life flows through.
Come to the waters if thirsty. Sunrise the morning
awakes, a new day.
Come to the water—take, I pray.
Drink from the fountain of life each day. Filled with
living water day by day.
Moisture from heaven like the dew will wash and
cleanse as he flows through you.
Cactus in the desert draws of the dew, beauty in a dry
land, beauty.
Like cactus in the desert, you must be full of living
water, full of the Spirit,—Jesus is he.
Full of compassion as he flows through you;
full of mercy washed by the dew.
Full of his grace, he sustains you. Precious pools of
water, he sustains you.

Scripture references: John 4:14, 7:37–39

Calendar full, days set aside, time scheduled in, appointments, meetings dinners lunches, the days full, summer to winter spring to fall, years pass, was the time well spent, were good choices made each day, reflect, how can I make the most of each day. Should one set aside time for the one we don't see. The Lord waits desires to spend time with his family, quality time in his presence choose well only so much time.

Precious Gift

Lord, I feel sad today. Have I missed what the Spirit
would say?
Have I taken time to come and pray, to wait in your
presence to hear?
You rush here and there, like birds of the air, flittering,
fluttering about—
no time to get quiet, no time taken out to wait on me
this day.
No time to relinquish your will, your way.
You've made a wrong choice; the day's gone by.
Time, precious—a gift to use.
I give you time; you must choose.
Life like a vapour soon goes away, so take time, my
child—come and pray.
Do not rush to get away. Linger here; hear me say you
can do nothing apart from me.
Come, I ask, take time out for me.
Programs, committees—all of man's plans, good
though they seem, cannot take the land.
You need my Spirit, my power, my plan.
Come to the Master; enter the land.
I give you the keys that you need.
I give you life, my Spirit feeds.
Yield and obey, take time to pray.
Dwell with the Master, come every day.
Rushing around all about town, my people they scur-
ry—oh, what's the hurry?
Still, sit still, my will fulfill.
Come to the Master, come as you will.

IN HIS PRESENCE

Sit by my side; for you I died.

I gave my life to end the strife, division, and hate.

A world of sin, defeated, heartbroken people need my

Spirit, my guidance, my love; they need the Holy God.

They need to know that I will go with them in trouble,

life; they will discover, uncover love, uncover me.

Tell the lonely, the lost, of my love—tell of me.

Come, be filled; I will pardon.

Come, be nourished, feed.

My Word sufficient; my grace, my hand extended,

reaching. Uncover love as I live in thee.

No time to pray—busy, you say? You hurry and scurry

all about, no blanket of love, no warmth.

My children empty, no time for me.

Look, see the lost, consider the cost: people, friends,

all could be lost.

I came to save, my life gave;

my hand is reaching to you.

Did you speak to that sister? Did you tell of my love?

My blanket of healing shall wrap around you; my

blood to cleanse, wash.

Cleansed and forgiven, my life was given to cleanse

the sinner.

Time is so precious—my gift to you. How will you

spend what I have given you?

Will you bury your talents, hide, I say? Will you leave

time in your day?

Consider how well you spend each day. Do you dwell

in me each day?

Do you read my Word each day? I give you time.

Will you come to me and pray?

Fun and excitement, tears of joy, like children at play

with new toys.

Busy, enticed with natural life, no time for the Spirit;
eternal life, hidden within, no time—what a sin!
A gift was given to men—gift of life, time on earth. Like
the flower I give you birth.
You grow tall and strong all day long to give new
beauty to the earth.
Give of your life. Give, I say. Give me time out of your
day. Commune with me, the Spirit would say.
Take the time to pray.

Scripture References: Proverbs: 27:1; Ecclesiastes 3:1–22; 1
John 2:17

Mother Goose, Goldilocks and the Three Bears, Little Red Riding Hood, Jack and the Beanstalk: fairy tales, passed down through the generations. Every generation passes on stories, giving insight to life in that time. The birth of Jesus—King of kings, the light of the world come to earth. Jesus, his life story, the miracles passed down through each generation—some might regard these as just fairy tales or good stories. People need a revelation of the Living Word: Jesus, Saviour, come to earth. Time passes quickly, eternity awaits. Let's us give more thought and weight to the Bible— the truth revealed within, life eternal given for man. Pray for wisdom and revelation to guide our lives— eternity awaits. Thank you, Lord, for your redemption plan. Amen.

Redemption Plan

Who is the man, nail prints in his hand?
Who understood God's eternal plan?
Was he God's Son, or just a man?
Was he the Christ, Saviour of man?
Now the story be told by those so bold;
boldly they spoke of God's son—
told of the time when he did come,
and later the cross where he hung.
Nail prints, scars, a crown of thorns,
the death on the cross—a life was lost.
Now men reject Jesus; they mock and scowl.
They don't understand the redemption plan,
nor do they see his beauty. The Son nailed to a tree.
Principalities, powers will all bow their knee.
Sin and deception blind people.
No time for Jesus, no time;
they mock, laugh, say how busy they are.
Time will come to bow to the Son;
his soon return—many will burn.
The price of sin we learn.
Now take a moment, reflect:
Do you remember what some did say?
"Come down from that cross, save yourself."
He could have called angels to rescue his life
when he hung on the tree.
Save yourself; come to me.
Come while the door is open wide.
Come to the table; with Jesus abide.
Sit with the Father in the throne room.

IN HIS PRESENCE

Come while you are able, life in bloom.
A flower you are in God's room.
Part of the beauty you see
is the love of Jesus reaching to thee.
Come while you are able; adorn his table.
Come with praise fragrance so sweet,
the fragrance of Jesus.
Others meet as you dine at the table, sit at his feet.
Much like the flower, life blows away;
petals fall, dying each day.
Soon the bloom is gone from the stem;
the life of the flower has come to an end.
Endings, beginnings, the cycle of life;
come to God's presence while you have life.
Come to his table while you are able.
Draw from his well water so sweet,
when you draw deep.
Pure and clean, no need to screen,
refreshing, quenching the drought in you.
Drink of the water your life through.
Flowers need water, they need the dew, they need
refreshing, as do you.
Beauty will blossom—eat, drink.
I welcome you.
Nail prints, scars, a crown of thorns—
you heard the message.
You were warned of the danger that awaits.
I came for the lost, the man in rags.
I came for the rich, all scallywags.
I came for mankind, the sick, the lame.
I came for all; I call your name.
Brother, sister, this is not a game.
This is the message I have for you:

Be careful, watch, consider—please do.
Watch for the one he sends your way.
Refuse not the Master his call today.
Refuse not the friend I send your way.
Mock not at the word he has to say.
Take a moment, consider his way.
He is a friend sent to you.
Did he speak truth to your life?
No excuse should you turn away;
no excuses come.
I welcome you—come and pray.
Come to the Master this very day
Jesus, life-giver, hear him say,
"I bore your sin, come on in."
Come, you're welcome, come follow him.
Jesus, life-giver, pardons your sin,
wipes all away—invite him in.
Into your heart, his Spirit imparts
life eternal, he imparts;
lives forever in people's hearts.
Heart of the Father reaching to you,
heart of love calling, waiting, and watching all you do,
wanting to spend eternity with you.
Heart of the Father reaches to you—the choice is
yours you wear the shoe.
Ask him in, please do; abides forever, lives in you.
Never forsakes or leaves you, heart of love,
gift of God.
Heart of the Father, the Spirit imparts
his will in your heart—
talking, loving, living in you; ask him in, please do.
Heart of God living in you, ask Christ in—please do.
Live in my heart, my spirit renew; give me life—

I come to you.

Give me hope; I need you. Give me life; I desire you.

Give me grace to live for you; cherish each moment I spend with you.

Make the decision, the message has been given.

Make the decision to go to heaven.

Decisions, decisions—you must decide to ask him to come inside.

Knock, knock.

Is that your door? Is someone knocking at your heart's door?

Knock, knock.

Is he at your door?

Knock, knock.

Will you open the door?

Knock, knock.

Scripture references: Ecclesiastes 3:1–8; Matthew 24:37–44, 27:1–54; John 3:16–20, John 4:7–1; Acts 1:1–10, 17–23, 2:14–36; Hebrews: 3:7–15

Do we value time we're given time cannot be recouped valuable the hours only so much time. Interests, obligations, meetings, work fill the day.
Hard work
achievements, advances, so much to be concerned about. The days pass time gone, did we neglect to spend time with the Lord? Do we see of the need of the souls who pass your way, men who need the eternal plan. Temporal riches fame fortune, the stubble and hay burn away, souls need God's plan. We are rich with the fullness of the Lord perhaps more time in his presence for the lost, the beggar who knocks on our heart's door. Thank you, Lord for your eternal riches, may we truly share the heart of the Lord.

Rags To Riches

Lord, my heart heavy; my spirit does cry.
There is a sadness—I don't know why.
Times of heaviness, clouds around me, times of sor-
row, my heart wishing, wanting to be
counted worthy as I walk with thee.
Lord, give me wisdom; help me look with your eyes to
the heart.
I've been judgmental; the sin I saw, judged by
appearance, sin.
A man in good apparel, suave and debonair, came to
the table, given head chair.
The beggar in rags—who did care? Did they turn to
welcome him or offer a chair?
Rags to riches, you came to me wrapped in swaddling
clothes, king.
You are King—riches and wealth come to me. I was
that beggar,poor was I—rags to riches, you came by.
You passed through the crowd, heard my heart's cry—
rags to riches, wealthy am I.
Clothed with your Spirit, adorned by your love, draped
in mercy—naked, not I.
I am so wealthy—a beggar, not me. Once I was poor,
lived in poverty, wanted only what my
eyes could see, longed for riches, though temporal,
the silver and gold.
The houses, the mansions—stubble and hay, burned
in the fire, consumed that day.
On the day of judgement, all burned away.

Then I turned to good works of my hand, helped and
gave to those in the land.
Good works I excelled in—helped the needy, gave to
them. I did not know that would not do;
I tried so hard to work for you.
I did those things to please you, unwilling to sit, spend
time with you. I worked very hard,
my hands scarred; busy and bragging of the good I
do, wanted recognition, glory too.
Then spoke the Saviour: "That will not do—filthy rags,
works, won't do.
I paid the price to live through you.
Good your deeds, but that will not do. I need your
will—I need you.
I need your will, the works I'll do. I am the one who
dwells in you.
I give you the desire, my purpose in you.
I change the heart, will to live my life through you, to
admonish the truth in you.
I sat contemplating what to do—to yield to the Spirit in
all I do, to rise to new heights found in you.
To rise to victory in all you do.
You are Lord; I acknowledge you. I will serve my whole
life through. Today is a new day, a challenge to trust
and obey in all I do.
Yesterday gone, I cannot redeem. Was it wisely spent?
Did someone you redeem?
The life of a child perhaps lost in the stream. At times
we are so willing to walk our own way, willing to settle
for stubble and hay.
Rags to riches, Lord, I say—
clothed with your Spirit, wealth.

Now, the beggar may be someone's friend, someone
special in the end. Someone very dear.
Is he your friend? Is he an acquaintance? When will
his life end?
Is he a father or just a young man? Is he a neighbour
or a husband? Who is that man?
Did anyone say? Did he stumble across
your path this day?
Did you indulge, converse I say? Did you ask his name
or his hand shake?
Do you feel the hurts as your hand he takes? Beggar
in rags succumbs to the weight.
The pressure, sin. Does his heart ache?
I once knew a young man who needed God's plan. He
had a great future as he lived in the land.
Gifts of God were in the plan, but deception and blind-
ness stole that young man.
He wandered away, from God did stray; chose the
wrong fork, choose the wrong path.
Wandered in darkness day by day.
God in his mercy spared the soul of that man
as others did pray.
Pleaded with Jesus, sat in prayer, held his name—
they really cared.
Wanted the best, for him to be blessed. Interceded
and prayed, clothed that day.
Sent the Spirit of God to soften the heart, to draw to
the Father, his Spirit impart.
Drawn by love, gift of God. Love, child,
in him be shod.
That young man—was he your son?
Was he someone's father, child so young?
Gone into eternity to live with the Son.

Prayer is a mighty force. Prayer is hearts seeking
God's course, seeking his will, his eternal way, yield-
ing and wanting God's very best. The plan of God
others bless.
Now I have learned a lesson, hard it may seem—my
eyes open, I awake from a dream.
I dreamed of that young man, his precious soul caught
in turmoil on hard soil,
caught in the fingers of sin—blinded, deceived,
no life within.
Within was turmoil—unrest, you see—
wanted to believe.
Found out how difficult that could be,
so the deceiver blinds.
Now light will come as you yield to the Son. Believe in
Jesus, the only way to heaven,
one way to God. Believe the Word you have heard.
Believe the truth, the Word of God; with the gospel
your life be shod.
I want to tell you, Jesus is the way. Build your life on
what the Word does say.
The Word of truth given each day shall prepare the
ground, for the trumpet will sound.
You shall be waiting and living for him—guided by
God, his life within.
Waiting for the sound of the trumpet blast—the Lord
will return, come at last.
Come for his church, his bride of love—adorned and
clothed by grace from above.
Now remember the beggar and what you used to be;
give him a hand, the glory to see.
Welcome the beggar to sit, offer; there is a place.
Every beggar is welcomed, taken from rags to glory.

A place at the table, a chair maybe.

Were you that beggar? Was there a chair for thee? Did Father turn and welcome thee?

Were you that beggar? Not rich were we. We have gone from rags to glory;

clothed with God's Spirit, wealthy are we. Love is a precious gift given for thee.

Never was a beggar not welcomed by me. Welcome the homeless, the needy.

Welcome the outcast, for you see, many a beggar came to me.

I shared my life, given for thee. Now Lazarus was a beggar; no wealth had he.

He begged for crumbs from the rich. Wanted to be a blessing, did he.

In the bosom of Jesus, the rich man could see the beggar Lazarus, arms around thee.

The rich man lost his wealth in eternity— separated was he.

There was a gulf one could see—gulf separated.

No man could cross; the life had ended—all was lost.

Now begged the rich man, pleaded did he, "Send someone to my brothers,

tell them to believe and turn from sin. I pray, tell them, so they will not burn."

Though trouble surrounds, you're engulfed in the flame, remember Jesus—call on his name.

Call while there is time; eternity awaits, forever with Jesus his life to gain.

Don't be like the rich man, refusing to believe, for your time will come—this earth you will leave. All with vanish, fade away.

You will stand before the Lord come judgement day.

You will stand before the Saviour; you will hear him
say, "Child, I remitted your sins, washed away, for
under the blood you did stay washed
and cleansed every day.
Asked for forgiveness when you went astray;
accepted my plan, my way.
Another did not repent, refused my call the correction
I sent. Refused the ones I sent their way. Refused to
heed my will, my way. Refused a crown,
all stubble and hay.
No repentance or forgiveness, no sorrow for the sin,
no desire for my life within.
Rejected my name, my love, my blood. Refused to
acknowledge the God of love.
Now where are the pearls I gave to you? Did you bury
them too? Pearls of wisdom to draw you; pearls of
love I sent to you. What a beautiful necklace
you threw in my face.
Rejected my grace, rejected my all; from salvation you
did fall—refused to answer the Master's call.
The end of these ponderings, end of these thoughts.
I ask you a question: Have the Lord you sought?

Scripture references: Isaiah 64:6; Matthew 11:28–30; Luke
14:7–14, 16:19–31

Morning Beauty

I saw a blackbird nestled in a tree. I heard the song he
chirped for me.

I saw his beauty, black as could be. The Lord brought
the blackbird; he sang a song for me.

I am your Father—rest in me; be like the bird nestled in
the tree.

Hidden in the branches, out of sight—

sheltered, dwelling close to the trunk, protected from
the wind and sun.

Nestled in the branches, child, you must be close to
the trunk;

only then will you see the care of the Master, his hand.

Special are my children, much like the blackbird I
caused you to see.

Wake in the morning, rise early, see the beauty
of the morning.

I will speak with thee.

I place my mantle that others may see the love of
Jesus in child such as thee.

You must yield your life, hide in the branches of the
tree; I see the heart and what may be.

Hide in the branches; draw nigh to me. Wait, listen—
then you will see

the anointing of love abiding in thee, the anointing of
Jesus full shall you be.

Much like the blackbird, you need me. He needs the
shelter of the tree, child.

Like the blackbird, child, you need me.

Ravens fed Elijah, filled and nourished was he.

I sent ravens, food they brought.

I am the one who feeds food from heaven. It is all from
the Master; he will feed thee.
Alone and weary at times, come nestle in the branches
close to the tree.
Sometimes in treetops the bird sits, being warmed by
the sunshine provided.
Out on a limb—child, be drawn back in the branches,
talk to me.
I know the strength of the limb that supports thee. I am
the one; I am the tree.
I know the limb, how strong it may be.
Wings to fly, take of the beauty, free and flowing in the
current of life,
strength and provision provided. When you are weary,
come rest.
Much like the blackbird in the morning, he flew to
the tree top; on the highest of limbs, there sat he.
Surveyed the beauty, all his eye could see—safe and
secure, he sat on the tree.
The beauty of the blackbird heights, much like an
eagle, though little is he.
Each is beauty created; each one is precious—
like you are to me.
Many blackbirds, child, many children dwell in me.
I call you, children, to nestle; stay in the branches next
to the tree.
Nestle in the branches—shelter there. Children of
beauty, love covers thee.
Come near to the tree, nestle in safety, nestle in me.
Nestled in safety, love covering my children, love
covers thee.

Scripture references: 1 Kings17:1–9; Luke 12:23–32; John 15:1–6

The journey through life can be very difficult at times: stress, heartache, great sorrow and pain, also times of joy and wonderful victories. In difficult times, our foundation is the Word—the Living Word, never changing. We listen and read, and many voices speak. The Living Word gives peace, life, wisdom in each situation. Wisdom found in the Bible, the Book of Life—our hope must be in the unchanging Word that brings peace, courage, hope, and faith to our lives. Let's remember to open the Book of Life and heed the instruction within. The eternal found in the pages, the strength of our lives found in the Word. Love never fails. Jesus is the Living Word.

Tattered Pages

Tattered and torn, the pages are worn. Fingers have
touched; the book was clutched. Thumb through the
pages for direction, finding the passage to help.
No dust on the cover you shall discover; used for each
day, not hid away.
Unravel the mystery of life—the Book of Life,
given for each day.
Book of adventure through the travel of time, each has
a passage as life unwinds.
No other book, not another, took down from the
shelf—help yourself.
Many an author, may I say, gifted and blessed
as my hand.
I'm not the author—the thoughts are not mine.
I've been gifted with life divine.
Each word penned is love from a friend. I am just a
vessel; my hand I do lend.
I've only discovered, wealth uncovered—the Bible,
just take a look.
Look in the pages—wealth through the ages;
learn of children gone before me, now with the
Master seated be.
I learn of their faith, their story. Peter and Paul,
who answered your call.
Matthew and Luke, Mark I read, John the disciple
loved by thee.
Many children, like the stars in the skies,
gifted from thee.

Promised children as they look to thee, descendants
as many as the stars in the skies. Countless genera-
tions follow; many have walked close. Many through
trials, Lord, I see.
I see the miracles: When they crossed the sea,
the waters parted, held back.
Manna from heaven, bread was given. People of
God—people trusting, following, bending and bowing
to the Lord.
Trusting in Jesus—following.
Generations shall tell of the Lord. Now when you are
weary and fail to believe,
look in the Bible—faith, receive. Take from God the
word you need; come and receive.
A doctor, a lawyer, a man of the world—foolish to
some, the words they heard.
The thinking of man can't understand foolish to the
natural man.
Look close in the mirror; come, draw near. You see the
outward how man does appear— outward appearance
in the mirror.
I look in the eyes deep inside you, see the colour.
You see the size; I see the soul as only I know. I see
the longing, the empty hole;
you see the hands, the palms of man. You see the
frame; I see the lame.
Lame beggar to Jesus came; healed the lame man—
whole was he.
I see the beggar hidden in thee—begging for love,
reaching for me. Crying and hurting— this I see.
You see the circumstance; you see the cause—
misunderstood, judge, applause.

Now I see a deep, empty, dry well. No living water
flowing; no refreshing to wash thee. Deep is the hole,
and empty are thee. Well of life—this you need;
river of life, flow out of thee. Look in the mirror.
What do you see?
Do you see a scar on the face that be? Do you see
beyond the flesh?
Do you see more than the rest? Do you dwell in that
spot, take another thought?
Reflect how the years have changed thee. Silver the
hair on your head.
No longer youth in the mirror; you see wrinkles and a
frown line.
Smiles and tears, travels through time, lines on the
face with the passage of time.
Look in the mirror—I call to mine. The fine lines of
change show on your face.
Smiles the heartaches erase; tears of joy run down
your face.
Child, you soon end the race. Race to the finish,
shoes worn.
Tattered and broken through many a storm;
grip is loosed in the storm.
Worn are you, child, in the storm. Now at the end of
this race, many are cheering.
They see your face; many are shouting,
"Finish the race. Enter the gate, heaven awaits."
I sat before Jesus; my life he eases. Eases the burden,
wipes my tears.
Many a time through the years, the Lord
wiped my tears.
Now my life is over; I've grown old. Silver my hair—
no colour there.

My body is weary; a new one awaits as I cross over
into heaven's gate.
No pain, no sorrow in my tomorrow. No tears
in future years.
I dwell in a mansion given to me; walk
on the streets of gold.
I ask you, dear neighbour, to forgive me. I ask you,
my family, friends—
may you forgive where I have failed Forgive all my
faults, shortcomings you see.
It took a lifetime to grow in me. I need changing my
heart, you see.
I needed love to grow in me. I need Jesus
a blessing to be.
I may have failed when I walked with you;
may at times have been untrue.
Many a day I lived through unyielded, unwilling to live
for you, live like the Master would. Have me do life
unselfishly, thinking of you. Live so my life would
beckon you.
Beckon, Jesus, a desire in you.
Forgive me, dear friend, my life I now lend. Lend to
Jesus, my precious friend.
I cannot partake; sin I forsake—
many lives are at stake.
I lend my life, my gift to you.
May I live always, give unselfishly,
that others may live.

Scripture references: Psalm 32:8–11; Isaiah 42:16; 2 Corinthians
2:14; Colossians 1:9–13

In the storm, when your eye can't see, trust in the Word, the Living Word. Who can calm the storm the raging sea? The impossible, leave to the Lord. Many hardships in life, many impossible situations we find ourselves in, having exhausted all possibilities. Know the victory is in the wisdom and strength of the Lord. Battle after battle, trail upon trail, victory is in Jesus. Listen, obey each command of the Lord; follow close, hear him speak, trust, obey. Love the solid rock. Jesus is love, and love never fails Be wise—let wisdom guide.

Weeping in the Land

I hear weeping and crying in the land. I hear the
groaning of man.
Saints crying out, hearts torn in pain. I hear crying,
and Jesus reigns.
The tomorrows are held in my hand; the day
passes—perhaps you have failed to see.
Though trouble surrounds, though the battle is hard
and hearts heavy:
Do you truly fail to see? Jesus fails not.
The trouble, overwhelming thoughts—how can I truly
overcome? I yield, trust the Son. The battle cry has
sounded in the land; take your position
under his command.
A war is raging, fighting in the land; the true battle is
won under his command.
The saints are fighting, waging war;
the spirits are surrendered to the command
of the Lord.
The enemy advances on every front, but the victor
is Jesus—the truth, blunt.
No army wins a war on its own; the choice is to wait
on the Lord.
In the thick of battle, wait to hear the word and move
in the direction of the Lord.
Pride has no place in the warrior's heart; flesh—
the armour that surely falls apart.
The sticks and stones of the flesh will bring bondage,
not victory in life.

The battle cry is heard in the land. Rise up under his
command.
Seek direction; listen for his voice—follow, obey,
rejoice.
You will not falter or fall prey to the advancing army as
you obey.
The scene looks hopeless; the battle appears
to be lost.
Love counted the cost—victory was won on the cross.
So falter not; trust what you see. All truth
is in the Word.
Love never fails; love prevails— shelter and provision
given. Count the Lord trustworthy. Trust in your maker;
trust in the Lord. The battle his—victory assured.
The saints march on; the war rages.
The victory is now seen on faces—the quiet
confidence of saints in the Lord.
Saints at war, the followers of love surrendered
to the Lord.
Followers, victorious saints at war—weeping
turned to joy.
Faces, victory smiles, the end of the journey—
the long, hard mile.
Faces, victory smile—the army of love,
the advance of peace.
The moving of love in a land not at peace;
the power to love the land does sweep life with
vision—the hope of men the true picture at the end.
The end of the trauma, the end of the day, when saints
cry out, "Father, have your way." The heart in rebellion
now at bay; the saints have another victory for the day.
The day in the life of war—the unseen enemy of souls

stealing the eternal the true gold. The gold, the crown
of men is made up of souls—stand, fight for them.
Fight the good fight of faith and leave not undone.
Fight the good fight of faith—leave no soul the chance
to escape.
Victory is love moving in the land; follow close each
command.
Heed each direction; move in his will—obey,
see the victory.
It is the will of the Lord all would come to salvation
and receive the true gift—
eternal life, gift of a loving, gracious Father
who foresees all, knows all, and can instruct all in the
path of life.
If you are at the crossroads of life, the decision is now
before you—
choose not to falter in indecision,
for saints and sinners alike pass to eternity, perhaps at
an unsuspecting moment,
no awareness of the proximity of time.
The precious hours have now passed, the hour clock
out of sand, the time runs out, the end of time.
Check where you stand and remember the hours,
the hands of time.
Do you know the sand that remains, or the time to the
last grain?
The hour approaches for each man.
Have you a grip on the sand?

Scripture references: Joshua 1:9; Psalm 9:9, 34:17, 91:1–16; Matthew 6:34; 2 Corinthians 10:3–5; Ephesians 6:10–18

The Bride

Success in life takes much preparation; nothing falls
out of the sky or magically happens.
The magic is found in preparation, hard work,
diligence—not just mere luck.
No genie to grant wishes. Time cannot be redeemed,
so we must be vigilant of the time given each one—
let's not waste this gift.
We prepare for meetings, special occasions,
weddings, holidays—
any worthwhile endeavour takes diligence, hard work.
Have we considered preparing for the eternal? We all
face eternity, the return of the Saviour.
Do we anticipate and prepare for it? Are we prepared
to meet the Lord?
Surely the bridegroom comes.
Life, like marriage—great victories, small squalls.
The bride of Jesus—what will it be?
Clad in white garments—no stain or wrinkle,
no blemish on the garment—
a bride pure and holy, washed.
Like the virgins the bridegroom went to meet, they
gathered their oil, got to their feet, prepared and ready
the bridegroom to meet.
"Give us some oil," the others cried. "We've not
enough," oh, they sighed.
"We'll give you no oil," the others replied.
"We ask that you give, enough there is; give of the oil
of your lanterns bid we."

IN HIS PRESENCE

Watch and be ready; the oil we need. In search of the
oil, they did toil.
They fussed and fumed, their oil consumed.
While they were searching for oil, the bridegroom
came—ready was he.
He came for the bride; the lanterns he saw, fueled and
ready—they answered his call.
Into his chambers the door was shut, away with the
bride—the others sighed.
No oil for the lanterns, no oil I say—
not prepared that day.
The bridegroom is coming; he is on the way. Fill your
lanterns—prepare today.
Fill the lanterns, be a light; he looks for the lanterns
and sees the light.
Fuel in the lanterns full; the bridegroom is coming and
calling to thee.
Prepare for his coming; dress in white,
clean garments, no spot—white.
No spot or wrinkle—cleansed by the blood, covered.
Full of the Spirit, full of light, full of the Word—he may
come in the night.
Fill your lantern, let it shine bright. Fuel the lantern;
the light he sees.
Prepared for his coming, the bridegroom will see.
In search of the bride is he; ready and waiting you
must be when he comes for the bride.

Scripture reference: Matthew 25:1–13

At times we struggle to believe that our prayers are heard, or that prayer makes a difference in the circumstances and trials we face. The trials are long and hard, thus we struggle to believe in the goodness and faithfulness of the Lord. Perhaps our wavering faith is due to a lack of time in his presence, in the Word, and in submission to the Lord—to know mercy and love, the one who gave his life. Let faith grow, be nourished and fed. Draw close and let the Lord speak; spend time in his presence. Let love lead, guide; help us to trust and believe love never fails.

Substance

Faith is the substance of things hoped for. Faith is the
courage to trust in the Lord.
Walking in truth, not deception; truth is Jesus,
his Word.
Call on the Master; his sheep hear his voice. Pray in
the Spirit; in Jesus rejoice.
Seek out the Father; seek Jesus the Lord—to the Holy
Spirit yield.
Please the Father; faith pleases him.
Precious promises given to men. Precious are the gifts
that come from him.
He rewards those who diligently seek him, diligently
seek his face. No respecter of persons is he. The faith
of the Lord given; when you pray, Jesus believe.
Faith moves mountains—trust and believe. Weak say,
"I am strong."
Wait on Jesus; bask in his love.
Know the Father; touch his heart. Stumble, not say it's
too hard to believe; from Jesus receive. Remember the
mustard, how small the seed—a small faith growing
each day as you yield your way. Faith grows, love
flows, growing in power for those who believe.
The eye cannot see but the spirit perceives, so trust
the Lord, choose to believe.
Faith moves mountains, crosses seas, builds bridges,
as you believe.
Leave behind the doubt and fear; say, "Lord, I trust
you. I choose to hear."

Jesus will whisper in your ear, tell you secrets as you
draw near.
Now wait for the Master to reveal his plan. Wait on the
Lord—his Word, understand.
The Word of truth living; each day the living Word,
hear what he will say.
People need Jesus. Yield your way; walk in victory day
by day.
Walk in the Spirit, hear him say, "I direct your way day
by day."
Jesus, he cursed the fig tree; the disciples later did
see the fig tree shriveled—dry dead.
The Word spoke and cursed the tree;
death did they see.
Spoke to the mountain, calmed the sea—great faith
the Lord had.
Many disciples follow him.
Many times we sink; don't walk on the water. Trust in
him. Learn to wait; change the fate.
The sea dried up; a wall of water backed up a pathway
dry—the Israelites walked away.
Peter jumped out of the boat—eyes on Jesus,
take note.
Walking on the water to Jesus we see; out stretched
his arms—held out to thee.
Sand castles shift and fall. The rock is solid on
Jesus—call.
Doubt not the Master his Word. Faith is substance
given to thee. Ask what you will; abide in me. Abide in
truth, his life. Ask, believe, come, receive—the will of
the Father, given for you.
Your will, your prayers unanswered? Listen, seek
Jesus, his will. Each day hear the Lord speak.

The will of the Father, prayers heard, the voice to my
saints very clear.
Listen closely, lend your ear, bow in submission, to
Jesus draw near.
Faith moves mountains, lives change. Call on Jesus—
call on his name.
Prayers answered, his life proclaim. Call on Jesus—
use his name.
Chariots of fire, angels at hand—battle,
fight at his command.
The Word of the Lord given to you—trust, obey,
breakthrough.
The force of evil will hinder you; use your warfare
armed anew.
Battle the powers of darkness—intercede, pray each
day. A light will shine; Satan will flee.
Bind powers, principalities.
Fast, pray, yield your way. Believe the Lord each day.
Fast, pray, yield your way. Believe the Lord each day.
Strike not out at another. Strive not with your brother.
The body is one, must yield to the son—unified, the
job will be done.
Only a portion given to you; only part of the
picture you see.
I paint the picture as you believe and keep coming.
I change thee.
A picture of beauty, a scene of love—Jesus paints,
intercedes, the prayers of his saints.
Do not faint; paint the picture his way.
You're a child—crayons you had, a picture to
colour each day.
Some colour beauty, a grand displayl sometimes
slothful, scribble away.

No real interest—wanted to play. A real mess,
no beauty—that's why I must paint for thee.
I choose the colour; the brush strokes are mine.
The scene unfolds as with me, you dine.
The picture perfect, the Master does paint.
Come, do not faint. When your will is to follow, to seek
my plan, the power will be given.
As you pray, I paint. Love moves mountains;
love parts seas.
Faith is believing when you don't see. Calling those
things that are not as though they were.
The sheep his voice do hear.
God is not a man that he should lie; blessings
promised as you abide. Stay close to his side.
Some men say, "Do this or that," but perhaps with the
Lord you should chat.
He gives you discernment. Seek his face. Come to his
table; he's set a place.
Your name written in the Lamb's Book of Life—
your name there because he paid the price.
Gave his life for your sins, and with his blood your
name written in.
Call those things that are not as though they were.
The voice of the Lord, his you hear.
My sheep hear my voice as they draw near. Draw from
the water—pure, living water flow in you— washing
and cleansing out the debris.
Nathan dipped, followed the word given him. He could
have doubted,
gave way to sin and refused to be cleansed. The voice
of the Lord came through:
Men spoke and said, "Dip in the Jordan, the muddy
water." How foolish did this appear!

How many times your wisdom, not mine? How much
self gets in the way?
Listen closely—yield, obey—what Jesus the Lord by
the Spirit would say.
Say not, "How foolish I'll be." Don't let pride steal from
thee. Did not Jesus part the sea?
Say, "Lord, I will receive." Just listen for the Word to
speak the Living Word.
So sit at his feet.

Scripture references: Numbers 23:19–20; Matthew 14:22–33,
17:20–21, 21:18–22; John 15:1–17; Ephesians 6:18;
Hebrews 11:1–6

We see through a glass darkly—much hidden, unclear.
Man has knowledge, forms opinions, makes
decisions, passes judgement.
Who has perfect wisdom and knowledge?
Who understands all things?
Therefore, let's not be wise in our own eyes but inquire
of the Lord—he is wisdom and justice.
Final judgement lies with the Lord, who is just, wise.
The Word of life knows all, sees all; therefore, let men
draw counsel, wisdom from the Living Word.
Man—not as wise as some would dare to think.
Justice comes from the Lord, maker of heaven and
earth. Let true justice and wisdom rule.

Scale of Justice

Rock, paper, scissors—the game is played
Rock, paper, scissors—a simple game.
Who will trump the hand you see? Rock over scissors,
scissors over paper.
Laughter, glee—who knows what hand will trump
the three?
Rock over scissors—foolish game. Games such as
checkers, children play.
Not too difficult, child's play—oh, the games
children play.
Grown, no longer children, the games of children no
longer play—no games, changed ways.
No checkers, no chess—put away. Come, follow me.
Trump card or an ace up the sleeve, I trump all cards,
the deck.
I see each move before thee—what will it be?
Men not as wise as some do seem.
I know all seen, all the unseen. I am wisdom;
I trump the king.
I know all the moves—not caught unaware.
Man has knowledge, but what do I care?
For I am wisdom. I see all the moves; I care about
justice, life in you.
I am a just, loving God. Justice prevails—I weigh the
scales, justice prevails.
The scales of justice prevail.

Scripture references: Proverbs 8, 11:1, 16:11-21, 33, 20:23;
Amos 5:24

Thank goodness for navigation, Google maps to pinpoint a desired location. What a great tool to keep one on track and arrive on time—not lost searching for the right road. Maps, cities, streets—all laid out, the modern touch. Places to go, direction not clear—bad roads, dead ends, a nightmare, lost, not clear the way. We depend on maps to guide, but the guide to life eternal has been mapped too. The Bible, the Living Word, guides us through rough terrain; on the narrow road, direction we gain. Road of life or another road we take, perhaps time to search the life road map— the guide, Jesus, hear: follow, obey. Destination sure. Thank you, Lord.

Right Road

They danced in the sunshine, children at play; they
came to his table, knelt to pray.

They came to minister, worship, pray. Lord God, you
are worthy.

We come, pray; we need your fullness—empty are we.
We need your life, need Jesus, all that he be. Friend,
brother is he; Master, Saviour all, provider, redeemer—
Jesus is life eternal flowing.

Child, when you are weary, come, turn from sin—
come, pray.

Little children, come to my presence—come, pray.

Filled with mercy, covered with love, arms around you,
love from above.

Eat at my table, drink. When you are nourished, time
out to play, but come to my table.

Remember each day to sit with the Master. You hear
him say, "When you are weary, come, pray. Come to
me, children, take time—filled and nourished,
you may play.

Warmed with the sun, kissed by the dew;
flowers, children, much like you, they need the
moisture their life through.

Child, you need Jesus, and drink must you.

Drink of the waters flowing for you; flowing life, your
spirit renew.

Filled with his life, moisture, much like the flowers—
they need the dew.

Tended and cared for, he loves you. Nourished and
fed, life he gives.

Eat at his table; sit, I pray. The Master is waiting to
greet you each day.
I saw a robin early this day; he flew by my window
then flew away.
Don't be like the robin; come, sit, stay. Come, dwell,
don't turn away.
Sit at my table, sit.
Talk with the Lord; he guides your day. Be not like the
robin—he flew away.
Flew by my window, did not land; I looked for the
robin, but he flew away.
Come, children, let me lighten your load.
Come, children, I know the road.
You travel in darkness, carry a load; weary,
don't know the road.
You need someone to guide. Sit for a moment,
child, unload.
Your baggage is heavy; I'll carry the load.
Fears, frustrations, a heavy load hurts,
disappointments— you carry a load.
Leave all your parcels by the road; I'll carry your
burden, take your load.
Come walk with me. I will guide—turn, follow. Come,
there is a garden I want you to see.
Come, walk with me. Safe in the garden, under my
care; filled and nourished, your load I bear.
Play for a while, child; rejoice, dance in the sunshine,
heed my voice. I warn of the dangers;
I will shelter thee. I see things you do not see. My eyes
are open, watching.
I am your Father, arms around thee. Time to sit, time
to be filled and nourished,
time for healing scars. Times of refreshing you need.

Times of weeding—I am the gardener; rested and
nourished, I care for thee.
Walk on the path I have chosen.
I know the way—come.
I am your guide; I stand by your side.
Come, talk a while.
When you are rested, we'll walk a mile; travel the road,
I'll carry the load.
I am your God; I know the road. Narrow the road—
few travel the road;
not like the highway to hell—many a traveller, many a
person fall, hurt by the enemy.
Road to heaven I guide. Do not go on the highway—
it leads away, from heaven goes astray.
Many a turn there will be. I am your guide; I will lead.
Which road will you take? Which will it be? One leads
to heaven, the other a road of destruction—
hell a highway of sin and its penalty.
Stop. Change course. Come, turn from your sin—
turn away.
Come to the Master, hear him say, "I am the Lord;
receive this day.
Filled with my mercy, filled with my love,
road to heaven guided by love."
Road to the one who loves thee, Master Lord Jesus is
he. Road to heaven guided by love.
Life from the Master, filled with his love. I am your
guide, your map, Word of Life living in thee.
I guide your footsteps, watch over thee.
Come, child, let me be Lord, Master, God. Guided by
love, from sin set free.

Scripture references: Proverbs 14:12; Matthew 7:13–14,
11:28–30; 1 Peter 5:6–7

Busy, no time, lots to do: work, play, fill the day. Hours soon pass away.

How quickly the day draws to a close—time you cannot recover.

The question: Was there time set aside to abide in his presence, be filled with life and wisdom for the day?

Stubble, hay, burn away; the fruit of love you need.

Love bears fruit; love never fails. Fruitful lives as we abide.

No Figs

Be not like the fig tree—it bore no fruit.
In the distance, one could not see, but as they passed
by—no fruit.
Jesus cursed the fig tree, said let it be dried up from
the roots—no fruit do I see.
Fruit you shall bear; dwell in me. I see your life, watch
over thee.
Be not like the fig tree. When I pass by, let me see a
tree bearing fruit—a tree rooted in me. Nourished and
fed by the vine, roots down deep, placed in me—then
shall you bear fruit on the tree. Pruned, pinched,
cut back to bear more fruit. Close to the trunk your
branches, nourished and fed—my life flowing. Strong
and nourished, you shall bear fruit your life in me.
Look not like the fig tree—no fruit did it bear.
It flourished and grew, but nothing was there. No figs
on the branches—deceitful.
No food for the hungry—nothing. I cursed the fig tree;
it died.
Be not like the fig tree.
Listen, come, fruit you shall see as your roots go down
deep and you dwell in me.
I am your nourishment; I am He. Be not like the fig
tree—dwell in me.
Branches laden down with fruit, bending the bough,
growing in me.
Heavy and full, let your branches be
bending the bough.

Fed by the tree, bending the bough, heavy, clusters of
fruit, nourished.
Do not be like the fig tree.
Come to my presence; let others see fruit on the
branches—fruit.
Full are the branches as you dwell in me.
Be not like the fig tree, be not; it withered and died
when I spoke that day.
No fruit did it bear, nor life did it share—no food for the
needy, none there.
Empty yet pretty, no life there. Empty yet pretty, no
fruit did it bear.
Come to my presence and fruit bear as you dwell in
the vine under my care.
You will be pruned, cut back, to produce for the
gardener as you live in his care,
to a fruitful bough for others to see.
The care of the gardener—in his eyes you will make a
fruitful bough,
a fruitful bough dwelling in me.
The fig tree never blossomed, no fruit did it bear. Life
dried up—no fruit there.
No shade for the weary, no food. Be not like the fig
tree—deceitful.
Be not deceived: fruit you will bear as you dwell in my
presence under my care.
I'll prune, I'll pinch, I'll do a work there—
in my presence under my care.

Scripture references: Matthew 21:18–22; Mark 11:12–14; John
15:1–16

Did Jesus really rise again? Was he just another teacher, or the Son of God? Choices are made each day— some good, some unwise. To each the choice is given to believe accept the Word. Jesus is the risen Saviour, the light in darkness, the Son of God. Read, pray, seek wisdom. The Word is alive; Jesus is the Living Word. Pray for revelation and let the Living Word reveal himself. Love revealed in many ways—let the Word come alive in you. Listen, Jesus speak. Listen, the Word speaks.

Living or Legend

Living or legend? The question put to you. What are
the facts? Look, see.

Some say living, others nay form an opinion I will
guide the way.

Mohammed died, but did he rise?

Was Buddha a teacher wise? Do his followers heed
his teachings day by day?

Does Buddha answer when they pray? Does he give
direction, guide the day, words of wisdom does he
speak? Is he living? Does he hear? Can he counsel
when you draw near?

The shepherd, Jesus, living or dead? Read what the
Scripture said.

His sheep hear his voice; in him they abide. Draw
strength so they won't faint.

When they are thirsty, he refreshes their soul; living
water draw and know.

A counsellor, a teacher, comforter given; speaks direc-
tion, causes you to grow.

Only the living can speak to the dead. Only the living
can provide bread, living water when thirsty and dry.

Only the living can hear your heart's cry. Now is Bud-
dha living, or a teacher now dead?

Christ is an example to generations, a light in the
darkness to all men.

A lover of people, an example to them, but he reminds
that you can do nothing apart from him. Follow his
example, souls win.

Every command given to men: love the Lord; give all
to him. Die that I might live within.
Abide in the vine, his presence in you; apart from the
vine, nothing you can do.
He dwells in your praises; he speaks to you.
God is a spirit; he commands you be filled with the
Spirit—his life in you.
Many are filled, the Holy Ghost within. Filled with
Jesus, his life in them.
Singing praises, speaking with new tongues, praying
in the Spirit—life begun.
Begin today, be wise; others died but did not rise. Be
wise, for Jesus did rise.
Lives evermore to make intercession for you, so be
wise. Jesus did rise.
Disciples saw Jesus after that day—the day of resur-
rection from the grave.
The cross he bore for you that eternal life may be
given to you.
So why be foolish and say he does not speak? Go to
Jesus, his face seek.
My sheep hear my voice. Sing and rejoice—no more
blind, for the Lord is living in this time.
He speaks to his sheep, the anointing within
the well in him.
Well of living water quenches your thirst, satisfies the
hungry soul, makes whole.
Satisfied, drink when dry, eat when hungry,
feed the sheep.
The living Lord speaks, and the hungry his face seek.
Seek out Jesus—enter in prayer, dine at his table, a
place set there.

Come, feast at his banquet; with sinners don't sit.
What union, what fellowship if you refuse to sit? Just
another teacher teaching—heed the Lord, who desires
his sheep to feed.
So the question is: Can he speak today? Give him
room—let love bloom.
Bloom—fullness life abundant given to you.
Jesus feeds his sheep; come, sit at his feet. The sheep
need to eat feed; sit at Christ's feet and eat.
Life abundant gives you, life living the Word to you.
June 11, 1994

Scripture references: John 10:1–18, 11:25–26, 15:1–17; Romans
8:26; Ephesians 6:18

There is a time and season for everything: time to plant, time to harvest. Like the farmers who plant and harvest the fields, there is a time to harvest the souls. Lives come and go; time is of the essence. Let love lead the way, and send labourers to harvest the souls torn and beaten by the harsh winds of life.

Harvest

I arose in the morning, frost on the field; early the
storm, the crops shall not yield.
Destroyed in the battle, the foe had come. Battle for
souls as they rise to the Son.
Battle to yield, battle begun, to yield to Jesus, the Lord
God, the Son.
Harvest is near, the grain is bent.
Snow and frost the storm sent. Under the weight of
the heavy snow, touched by the frost,
the grain no longer grows. The seed's been damaged,
bitten, touched by the frost—not gathered. Hail and
winds, snow and frost, bend the stem—much is lost.
Lost are the souls through the storms of life; many are
hurt, many in strife.
Many deceived, many scorn, embittered—results of
the storm.
Storms of life come. Broken and torn—I heal, restore
life anew in you.
Out to the fields the harvesters go to gather the grain
damaged by snow;
now warmed in the sun as the warm winds blow.
The warmth of the Spirit's love causes you to know,
blow on your life, end the strife, heal all the scars,
give new life.
I will warm and dry the cold in you, warm and
comfort—I'll heal you.
For the wind of the Spirit shall blow dry your tears;
I watch over you.

I see the hurt; I see through you. Warmed and dried as
the winds blow,
gone is the frost, melts the snow. The toil of the
harvest has begun.
Hard is the work, child, of the Son.
Toil you must; labour, I say. Repent and yield to me
every day.
Then filled and healed, the reapers must go out to the
field to gather the yield.
To glean each kernel left in the field. Each is precious,
a harvest it yields.
Glean the grain left in the field. Love is your labour.
The labour of love shall never fail; kind and patient,
never proud—the Word in thee.
Love never loud and boasting, haughty, or proud. Kind
and gentle, yielded, Lord God living in me. Love never
fails; love lives to gather the grain in the field, to gather
the crop its yield.
Labour of love, out in the field; labour of love, a
harvest it yields.

Scripture references: Matthew 9:35–38, 13:18–30; Mark 4:26–29;
Luke 10:1–32

Excitement in the air: hurry, scurry, gift wrapping, preparing
Time when family, friends return to celebrate the
Christmas season.
Children, laughter, gifts, paper, ribbons, and bows.
Some decline to come; presents left undone, disap-
pointed love ones are unable to come. Salvation a
gift—many tarry, don't partake of this gift of eternal life.
Come, partake, open the gift waiting for you. Salva-
tion—a free gift.
Come, receive—the gift awaits. Do you hear knocking
on your heart's door?
The gift of life waits. Love waits for you to receive.
Come while you are able.
Love waits.

Ribbon and Bows

Ribbons and bows, a package with pretty paper—
what can this be?
Ribbons and bows, a package still under the tree,
though it is not Christmas—that has long passed. The
parcel remains unopened, shaken and rattled.
What can it be?
Curious what's in it, I ask, "What could it possibly be,
so nicely dressed, carefully wrapped?"
Now the storm has passed; it did not last; delayed the
one for who it be.
Days, weeks, years have passed, but the present is
still under the tree.
When hope seems to have gone, you have waited so
long, doubting.
Will the time come when you can rejoice with the one,
chosen to sit, with family dine?
Choose to laugh—rejoice, I say. Time carries
on faith wavers,
looking each day for the blessed child, far away.
For storms come and time does pass;
faith wavers, teeters between the word and doubt.
Bang! A knock on the door, a loud shout
that one is here;
Come, draw near, rejoice my children.
The Lord is the present we wait for; he is the one who
knocks on heart's door.
Gift of love on that Christmas day. Saviour came to
wash sin away.
No toil or struggle; relax, rest—the Lord of wisdom
knows best.

He counsels his children: "Come to me. I have a gift
awaiting thee."
Present, gift, a package for thee.
Look to Jesus— the gift is he.
Loved ones come home—I call their name. Each one
gifted; not all the same.
Gifts I give. Call on my name; abide in life—in Jesus
Christ, the author creator of life.
Life eternal my gift to you. No matter the day,
come, I say.
A package, a parcel, ribbons and bows—what's in the
box? Who knows! Now open—see inside.
Would I disappoint? Would I lie? A beautiful gift
hidden inside.
The box full of treasures and blessings for you—open,
rejoice, laugh! Open the parcel.
Rejoicing and laughing when the lost come home,
do not waver—keep the faith.
Love ones, turn around—come home; at my table
dine.
Saving the gift, with ribbons and bows
on them bestow.
Give them the gift, hand them the parcel,
love's the way.
Gift much bigger than life: eternal the gift that awaits
the lost. Give the gift—it came at great cost.
Knock, knock! Has a loved one returned the gift?
Await the loved one's return. Loved ones, come home.
Jesus the Saviour calls, "Come home."
The gift eternal awaits your return.

Scripture references: John 3:16; Romans 6:23; Ephesians 2:8–9;
Revelation 3:20

What is your vision of the future? Perhaps fame, fortune, good success. Some plans are realized in time; others fail to succeed. When we are disheartened and fail to achieve, perhaps the path travelled is not the best path—the chosen plan of the Lord. Wisdom given to guide our way helps us follow the Lord. No vainglory or self-seeking ways will bring true, lasting fulfillment that is found in his purpose. On the path of submission, obedience brings us to the cross. In that plan, we realize love never fails, love knows best. Love—our rock and foundation. May we follow, obey the Lord, the living Word, the Alpha and Omega, the beginning and end—our lives found in him.

Designer's Plan

Am I not the great designer? Did I not form the world?
Who was Noah's instructor? Was it my voice he
heard? Was he bowed in submission?
Did he take time to pray? Did he listen for my instruc-
tion as he went his way?
Was the temple built on my word alone? Did I instruct
the placing of each stone?
Have you yielded to the Holy one?
Have you come to his throne, obeyed the scriptures,
his voice alone?
Did the times and the seasons bring changes
to your life?
Have you entered in division, confusion, and strife?
Have you been confused, your way lost?
Lost your footing, the foundation way unsure? Was it
built on the solid rock, cleansed by the Word?
Obedient and willing when my voice you heard?
You are a living stone; trust in me alone. Enter in
worship; pray around the throne.
Sometimes of the calling you seem unsure, indifferent,
unwilling, insecure.
Now the time has come, child—run to the throne
room, talk to the son.
Jesus, I need help today—lost and discouraged,
frightened, I say.
You're the master builder; your design I choose. I bow
in your presence; my life I lose.
I come for a cleansing, an anointing of love. Cleanse
and purify, wash me in your blood.

IN HIS PRESENCE

The times and the seasons, my mind reasons—
why the change in the season?
You need direction.
Each stone must fit—just like Noah when he
built the ship;
each piece was placed, the instruction clear, each
piece chosen. Listen, bring your ear.
Walls are torn down; the sand washed away. Footing
unsure, your future secure?
Now are you on the solid rock that stands the test of
time? Or is it your plan or mine?
Stones do tumble; a rockslide I see. Boulders falling
out of the path—flee!
Landslide, a cleansing tide, to remove all the boulders
the spots inside.
Remove all the garbage; remove all the trash.
Cleansed and anointed, my will at last.
I move the stones, the footing I pour. I build—
I am the Lord.
I am the Master; I design the plan. Is it my will,
your hand in mine?
Remove all your self- seeking ways; remove all
ambition that leads you astray.
Remove all the hurts with sin—don't flirt.
Come, child, I wash the heart—washed and cleansed,
enter in.
Lord, your hand—the plan you send.
So be careful to read the book; read the instructions,
take another look.
Are you where I would have you? Do you follow me?
Exalted by self, no glory I see. No triumph, no honour
in that for me.
Exalted by self, not my will for thee.

Living are the stones I have set in place, all about my
table—beauty graced.

No longer desiring to shine apart from me; no longer
desiring vainglory.

No longer in turmoil when at my feet you sit. Listen
and obey so the stones do fit.

One I place in public view to speak my Word, another
to minister—my voice must be heard.

One speaks to children, calls to their hearts; implant
vision, my will I impart.

Some are singers—they sing for me; draw into
worship those about thee.

The stones are placed with beauty and grace, moved
and directed, by me placed.

The walls are built, the foundation sure on the Word,
my voice clear.

Walls, living stones—come to my throne, instructed by
the Master, his Word alone.

Word of life living in thee; bow in submission,
your hands free.

Not tangled with the world and its entreaties;
not tangled but free in me.

Mountains fall, landslide—all removed when the
mountain does fall.

Fall of pride, lust of the eye, impure motive, insincere.
Not willing to lend your ear or waiting
my voice to hear;

not moving in power in this dark hour—alone and
impoverished hour by hour.

Alone and needy my people are; when you exalt
yourself, pride sets you ajar.

Ajar, not close to me, set ajar by sin. Set aside all of
your pride; listen closely by my side.

IN HIS PRESENCE

Some are called to the crowded sea;
some entrenched by sin.
Some push forward but not of me;
some unwilling to follow.
Lay aside all of that pride; sit close by my side. Adorn
the beauty that be beauty, love flowing. Beauty like
diamonds, cut and honed, no longer rough.
Polished stone, living gems, glowing in the son.
Run to the Father, his arms out held; receive Jesus,
receive the message he gives.
I want a willing heart, from sin depart. Depart and
return, from the Lord learn.
Learn not to insist, persist in your way, for your
unwillingness leads others astray.
Leads them into sin—no souls do you win. Win and
reap as my face you seek.
Seek love, seek power, seek the Word in this dark
hour. Seek and minister in love and power.
Seek and love the Lord this hour. The hour of power,
the season of change.
The course of your life the Spirit arranged; the heart to
follow after God provides a passage—
leads not others astray.
The passage through the darkness, the way of love,
the way of rejoicing—from sin set free.
The way of truth comes from me; the way of love, God
guides thee. The way of truth, living proof. Now Noah
the builder, he built an ark; trusted in the Lord
when all was dark.
Trusted in the cleansing flood, washed away the sin.
Righteous within, washed away the sin of the world,
took only the righteous that followed him.

Safe and secure inside the ark, the flood waters rose,
the sky was dark. No life, no land.
The designer's plan—nothing left living no dry land.
Two of every kind, safe just in time.
The clock of judgement, the story in time. Now the
earth covered by the flood.
A symbol to heed—be covered by the blood.
Cover over your sin, safe within the covenant—
the covenant of love.
Love—a covenant—Jesus died for you. The covenant
of love given for you;
covenant of mercy your life through. Covenant of love,
covered by the blood the blood of Jesus,
the love of God, safe inside—in Jesus abide.
Abide in his mercy; abide in his love—safe and secure
under the blood.
Covered by love, a multitude of sin; covered by Jesus,
the soul in him.
Covered ugly specks and spots, garment unclean;
in need of a cleansing from sin unseen.
Buried in the sea of forgetfulness as you repent;
under the blood, a covering sent.
Now was Noah the only righteous one? Or was there
righteousness in his sons?
The family of eight inside closed the gate safe—
secure in the ark from fear.
Fear and torment, the flood was sent. Wishing they
had more time to repent before the rain was sent. Now
is this a message for us to repent? Repent of your
sins, the spots deep within.
All ungodly thoughts of pride that lift you high;
rather, repent.

Time spent as unto the Master your life is lent. I give
you a gift—
will you receive, repent, and believe in order
to receive?
Receive the message that comes from my throne,
obey my Word when my voice is heard.
Obey and believe; come, child, receive.
Come, child, only believe.
Build in your Spirit the desire of love, build in a longing
to follow love.
Build in a measure of fullness; receive the measure of
strength when weak are thee.
Measures of joy—how deep can it be, the measure of
understanding living in me?
Empty or full, no longer your will. Come inside,
in the ark abide.
Ark of safety fed and taught you; need to repent,
learn a lot.
Filled and pardoned, beautiful garden; herbs and
spices seasoned by love.
Gardens need my Word heed. Garden of healing,
sin not breeding, no strange or bitter plant.
See the work of the army ant tunnels of love dug down
deep underground,
the furrows deep, buried away from the light.
Out of the picture, out of the limelight, underground
the ant works around the night.
Hard work to remove sin's dirt, remove underground,
the work goes round.

Scriptures references: Genesis:6:13-22, 1Peter2:4-7,
Matthew 7:25, John15:4-9, Jeremiah 9:23-24, Proverbs16:18,
Deuteronomy7:9

It's easy to become distracted. Life draws us in many directions. Staying on goal requires perseverance. Keeping on track takes discipline, hard work. Success is more than luck. Some would say, "You're a lucky guy," knowing not what makes one successful, the labour put into the endeavour to bring the results. Have you heard the expression, "Born with a silver spoon in your mouth"? Not many are born into such circumstances. Nothing worthwhile in life is easy; there is a price to pay: hard work, sacrifice, the road to success. The road before is blest when the Lord leads, preparing the way. Wisdom, strength, the Lord provides for our every need—just follow, obey, abundant life found in him. Let him carry your load, guide, provide the things you need for life's journey. Love is the answer.

On Track

The spirit of heaviness presses me; clouds of
discontent, Father. Anger at times rises in me.
I hear excuses; my eyes see many. Excuse the sin
within, fall away, go astray.
Fall, the enemy's prey, unwilling to come to you, ask
for a cleansing, to be washed.
Fail in every detail—a life of love, a train derailed.
Steel on steel, God at the wheel.
Many junctions ,many turns—the journey made.
The engineer learned to follow the track open to him,
to direct the train on steel rim.
Once on the track, don't look back; give more fuel,
take up the slack.
Open the throttle, pedal to medal; a race to be won,
heed the Son.
He gives you the fuel to run the race, fills with love
each tiny space.
How like a train we refrain, run the course,
set the pace.
Remember, endurance takes the race. Endure to the
end; hold on, friend.
Give heed, your life lend. Now your journey may be
long through the valley—the train travels on.
Through rough mountain terrain goes the train, to
snow-covered valleys, the silence is broken. Clouds of
exhaust, a trail left. The clutter, the clamour of steel on
steel, sparks fly, the rail dry. Sparks and vapour leave
a trail; the train gone now—clear the sky.
No exhaust, no vapour nigh, no clamouring, clanging
on the rail.

FAYE THOM

All is quiet, all is still, no shrill whistle—all is still.
Like the train, love tough terrain.
You hear the Lord refrain. Love carries on
the journey long.
Love blows on you. Love covers a blanket for you. You
need love on your journey.
Blow the whistle; sound the alarm. The clamour, the
clang of love carries on.
Give your best, do no harm. The snow melts; the
valley now warm.
Through green pastures the train travels on. Sound the
alarm, warn of danger.
Jesus must be no stranger. You need God's people—
no lone rangers.
You need his voice, heed. Get back on track.
The enemy attacked. You gave in—derailed by sin.
Now on the track, child, fight back.
No time to be slack. A race to be won
to meet God's Son.
Give heed, sow good seed, and with love for others,
plead—get back on track.
Give your best, take up the slack. The enemy fights;
he attacks to derail your life off God's track. Get back
on track. Watch out for the enemy's attack. Press in, a
race to win. Sound the alarm.
Sin within—need a cleansing to follow him.
Cleansed and pure, holy—on track, God you see.
"Follow me," Jesus speaks to thee.
The whistle blows. Good seed sow and spend time
with Jesus the Lord—know.
1992

Scripture references: Deuteronomy 5:33, 31:8; Psalm 119:133;
Isaiah 30:21

www.ingramcontent.com/pod-product-compliance
Lightning Source LLC
LaVergne TN
LVHW021349080426
835508LV00020B/2185